THE

CHEAP DATE

GUIDE TO

STYLE

KIRA JOLLIFFE & BAY GARNETT

UNIVERSE

This edition first published in the United States in 2008 by:
UNIVERSE PUBLISHING
A division of
Rizzoli International Publications, Inc.
300 Park Avenue South
New York NY 10010
www.rizzoliusa.com

Originally published in Great Britain in 2007 by
TRANSWORLD PUBLISHERS
A division of The Random House Group Ltd
61–63 Uxbridge Road, London W5 5SA
www.booksattransworld.co.uk

ISBN-13: 978-0-7893-1693-6
Library of Congress Control Number: 2007906227

2008 2009 2010 2011
10 9 8 7 6 5 4 3 2 1
First US Edition

Printed in China

www.cheapdatestyle.com

CONTENTS

TO THE MEMORY OF GEORGE MELLY AND ISABELLA BLOW.

INTRODUCTION

If you want to look amazing, cool and powerful, this is the book for you.

Cheap Date is a magazine about finding dressing up a joyous thing—not slavishly following trends or copying what celebrities are wearing, but drawing from everywhere and anywhere. So, inspired by the fact that most "style guides" are barking up the wrong tree, this is our attempt to put the mystique back into chic.

Our best claim to authority is that we're passionate about clothes. We've had huge amounts of fun playing with them. In fact, that's how our friendship and working relationship started — over piles of charity-shop hauls. How deep is that? Very! We enjoy clothes' meanings, functions, textures, patterns and fabrics, and all the accompanying adventure of rooting good stuff out, wherever that may be. Our advice in this book applies to shopping at department stores, yard sales, H&M, grandma's wardrobe and Prada alike.

Style is about an attitude of substance, spirit and confidence, which your clothes simply reinforce. Clothes can also be an incredibly empowering tool. If you feel you look good, sexy and unique, then anything is possible. It could take just a belt, or a hat, or a leopard print that reminded you of something Patricia Arquette's character in *True Romance* would wear. It's about daring, following your whims, being a bit adventurous, creating magic.

This book will put you in touch with different looks you didn't realize you had, give you a fresh perspective on the whole putting-clothes-on-every-morning thing, and show you that you've already got style—mountains of it, in fact.

WHAT MAKES SOMEONE STYLISH

Stylishness is elusive, yet everyone is innately stylish. It boils down to confidence about your appearance. One thing's for sure: There's no specific type of dressing that's more stylish than another. Redneck or royal, minimal or opulent, style — to state the bleedin' obvious — is in you. It is not something you can buy.

Stylishness in the Nuba Mountains of Sudan.

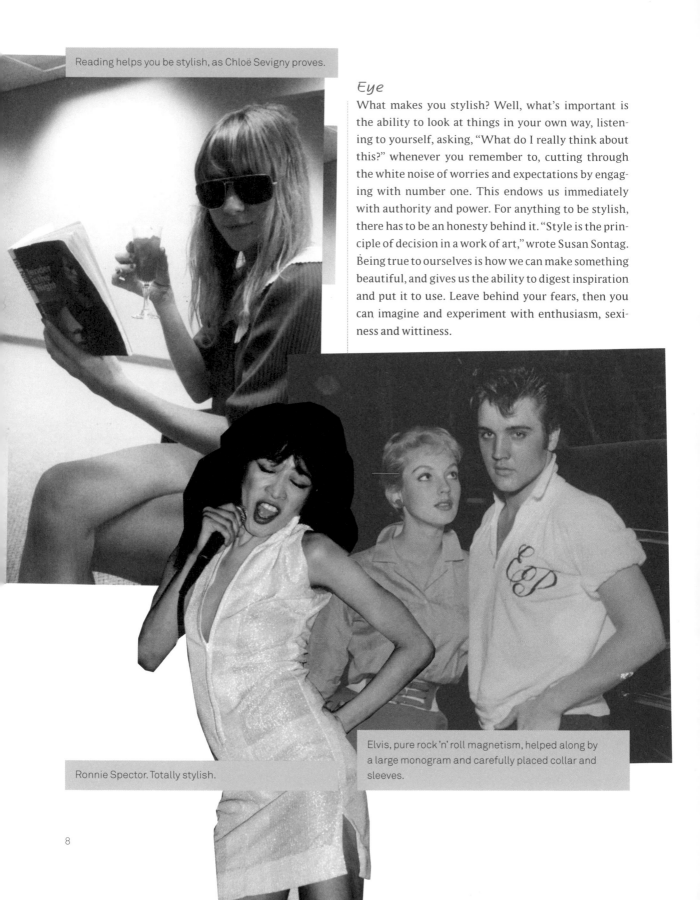

Reading helps you be stylish, as Chloë Sevigny proves.

Eye

What makes you stylish? Well, what's important is the ability to look at things in your own way, listening to yourself, asking, "What do I really think about this?" whenever you remember to, cutting through the white noise of worries and expectations by engaging with number one. This endows us immediately with authority and power. For anything to be stylish, there has to be an honesty behind it. "Style is the principle of decision in a work of art," wrote Susan Sontag. Being true to ourselves is how we can make something beautiful, and gives us the ability to digest inspiration and put it to use. Leave behind your fears, then you can imagine and experiment with enthusiasm, sexiness and wittiness.

Ronnie Spector. Totally stylish.

Elvis, pure rock 'n' roll magnetism, helped along by a large monogram and carefully placed collar and sleeves.

You

Take a swallow dive into the sparkling ocean of your personal culture. Your own complicated taste and its roots are plenty. The traditions behind your beliefs, heritage, culture, dreams, lifestyle and community are yours to be endlessly plundered or rebelled against, rooting you either way. Jean Cocteau said, "Style is a way of saying complicated things." Referencing what you know, instinctively or studiously, in what you wear reveals what kind of person you are and speaks to the like-minded. Stylish people care about what their clothes articulate about them. National costume and local history are a great source for meaningful originality and innovation. Your interests and passions, whatever they are, offer ideas, practical or not, for the little touches and alterations that give you your identifiable mark. People with a passion or a mission tend to be more stylish.

Bay's mother, Polly, through a child's doting eyes.

Kira's mother, Niki, on a pedestal, and the genius accessorizing of daughter Theodora.

Mum

A powerful tool is remembering formative style influences. Children are perceptive about clothes. You found certain shapes and colors pretty, and dressing up would have been an activity, with role-playing in costumes and fun with makeup and adornment. Kira's daughter, Theodora, age two, has the genius ability to wear a ton of pearls with a sailor outfit as well as dip her banana into tomato ketchup. You watched and admired what your mother wore and it formed templates in your imagination, with a magical, believing grasp of what clothes might say. The memory of this in later life becomes a basis of your style. Federico Fellini said, "Style is what unites memory or recollection, ideology, sentiment, nostalgia, presentiment, to the way we express all that. It's not what we say but how we say it that matters." Hark back to yourself as the most appreciative style observer that you were as a child, and use that same fresh eye now.

A certain grace

The mark of stylish people is that they don't have a problem with their appearance. They know their shape well and can accurately visualize how they look. Maybe this is as simple as making the happy choice to do this, maybe not, but it's interesting that anyone who isn't conventionally pretty can pull this off as easily as a perfect doll like Mischa Barton.

Karen Elson going about her business.

Aurora shows how easy it can be.

Phase

The style mojo (smojo) works and breaks with phases in life or your mood that day. Thinking about what you wear could be an irrelevant frivolity, especially when life events take over. Pregnancy and new motherhood is a classic wilderness time, style-wise. The smojo gets going with an inspiration flow, like a trip to an art museum, having basic clothes you're pleased with (see *The Basics*, page 31), being in love or reading this book…

Non-judgmentalism

Um, what else makes someone stylish? It helps to be accepting about what everyone else is wearing — unless they're in last year's heels. Just kidding! In the '60s there was an explosion of freedom that allowed everyone to be whoever they wanted to be and to experiment. Now, arguably, that's been eroded, and attitudes are more Victorian — the broke copy what the rich are wearing, and there isn't much deviation from the norm. It's natural to close ranks in a world that seems threatening, but let's do our bit for a more stylish society by staying open-minded. OK, so perhaps it isn't a crucial prerequisite to being stylish, but this is: We're not so afraid of being judged when we say, "Live and let live." It helps us accept ourselves.

The style stars realigned with The New York Dolls.

When you have a certain existential being, brilliant ideas slip in peripherally.

Effortlessness

Effortlessness can never be consciously achieved, but it is what makes someone stylish. Desperation kills it. The extremely stylish can wear something unflattering and have all the more panache for it. When you let go, pursue your muse, and have a certain existential being, brilliant ideas slip in peripherally; by playing with what you're wearing, you become, literally, marvelous.

Spirit

"Fashion is never having to decide who you are. Style is deciding who you are and being able to perpetuate it," said Quentin Crisp. Looking well turned out is one thing, but having style is much more ambitious and risky. Stylishness can help extra-sensitive people be themselves with the romantic and lovable protection of beauty. Putting a real spirit into what you wear, rather than just taste, requires both vulnerability and meeting people's gaze. It heightens your interaction with the world while you contribute something more of yourself to your environment.

Conviction

If you like following orders, this is ours to you: Stop it! This means ignoring TV makeover culture and fashion journalists who assume we're as unhealthily obsessed by trends as they are. It means not being freaked out if you're not rich, skinny, pampered and young. It means having the courage of our convictions, counting ourselves as precious and being able to harness how we look. It means being undiminished by pressures to conform and consume, standing strong, having the confidence to be beautiful and not being afraid to shine. Having style is political. Right on!

Standing strong.

Throwing yourself into a role. Here, Jeanne Moreau as a husband-killing, François Truffaut anti-heroine.

If you're drawn to her look, then "be" Janis Joplin: that's what it's all about.

12

Malcolm X described the zoot suit as "a killer-diller coat with a drape shape, reet pleats and shoulders padded like a lunatic's cell." By their dress, zoot suiters, mainly African-American, Filipino-American and Mexican-American youths, defiantly asserted themselves. The zoot suit riots happened in Los Angeles during World War II, when the Navy beat up anyone wearing a zoot suit.

Luella Bartley experiments with Kurt Cobain.

Jamie Lee Curtis as Megan Turner in *Blue Steel*.

Having style is political. Right on!

What makes not a jot of difference is where you live, your age, your weight, money, height, job, size or class. What can really help is having a cool job with a cool uniform. Mind you, a stylish person looks good in any uniform.

WHAT MAKES SOMEONE STYLISH?

I think it's originality; not following the herd; being a little bit daring; not trying to be fashionable. If you have your own style, you don't follow trends.

Rachel Weisz (actress)

The nature of the person. No other way. Style is something that makes a good vibration; a good relationship. It is a good way of being: smiling, receptive and being well received, and being happy.

Anna Piaggi (fashion director, Italian *Vogue*)

Most of all, I think it's confidence — if someone is completely confident in their style, then they never deviate from it because they feel comfortable in what they are wearing, and they know that it is true to themselves. Individuality is something that is so important to style that you can't really capture it or explain it. You are just completely unapologetic in the way that you look.

Mischa Barton (actress)

It is having a signature style no matter what it is, and finding it. Not following fashion; not being "of the moment."

Dita Von Teese (entertainer)

I don't think you can buy style. I think you can get it as you get older. It's like listening to jazz records that you couldn't listen to when you were a kid.

Róisín Murphy (singer)

The most stylish people don't take fashion too seriously. They like to be provocative to culture in their dress, and directly project their personality and fantasies onto it. Style is something each person has in their own way.

Zac Posen (designer)

I think stepping outside of the norm and mixing… it's all about the jumbo shrimp… Jumbo and shrimp — incongruent things going together. I suppose it's a desire to show an outward sign, propose oneself, mind over matter and the desire to seduce, and that doesn't mean it has to be sexy — it is artfully seductive. You have to have knowledge, and the really good, the really stylish people, can be so fluent with it, it's really erotic. I'm not ashamed to say I adore reading stylish people. Style is all about the gaps. It's about the spaces, it's individual and it can't really be replicated. It's the body; it's what goes in a twist and a turn. It's instinctive and inherent and it can portray an exciting mind.

Camilla Nickerson (fashion director, *W*)

I think thinking is stylish. Looking is stylish. Culture is stylish. I think you need to be inspired by something in order to look good. A poem, a picture of Wallis Simpson… I have an obsession with Wallis Simpson. When people talk about "style" and "stylish," they're talking about trends. She didn't have a trend. She wore clothes that looked good on her. I think style is about a person recognizing what their best features are. And if your best feature is a waist, wear a fucking waist. If you've got a good bust, go empire. I think it's about finding a mood that you keep to. Then everyone can identify with that style. I think what's unstylish is, as celebrities do nowadays, to borrow things from the PRs. They borrow, and it's so clear that the dress has just been sent. You can feel the bike delivery.

Isabella Blow (the late style legend)

Simplicity is the first thing. Second — the quality of the materials is very important in what you wear. Anything simple gains elegance when it's well made and good quality.

Lady Maria-Carmela Hambleden (grande dame)

When you can tell by looking at someone that they feel really amazing. People who are excited to be wearing what they're wearing, like little kids getting to wear what they want.

Beth Ditto (singer)

First, having a sense of your body. It's a personal choice, different for everyone. You know, a lot of people think because they get something fabulous it's going to look good on them, and that's not true. I think people can acquire style; I think that you can't ever acquire class. Style you can get taught, but ultimately it's how you carry it — it's something you either have or you haven't.

■ Kelis (singer)

To be slightly different from other people. I am not being snobbish about it. I think it is a gift. It can be helped a lot, mostly by parents. It can be a reaction to the dull and grey, or influenced by them if they are themselves rather hip. There is no accounting for it. It's often combined with a kind of restlessness. The belief in it. One can develop it, but not have it on thinking: "I want to be stylish." I would apparently have it, because I am told I do. I don't really care about how I dress — not very beautifully, they tell me. But with a certain panache, I suppose. I think panache is an important part of style. Oscar Wilde was the essence of style. A sort of deliberate martyr, which in itself is a sort of style. He could have gone to France the day before his arrest. He didn't. He sat there in his hotel, waiting for the two detectives.

■ George Melly (the late singer, surrealist, writer)

If a woman looks really stylish to me, not so much that I want to dress like her but that she just looks great, seems interesting and I want to talk to her. It's not the same as being secretly intimidated by someone. I think style has to be easy-going, or else it becomes something else, a show. It's good to pay attention to your clothes, it's not totally superficial – they represent you, you have to be comfortable with yourself in order to operate healthily and happily. Someone who wears clothing because it's functional can look totally fantastic, because the clothes are part of who they are.

■ Cecilia Dean (founder of *V* and *Visionaire*)

Attitude.

■ Bella Freud (clothes designer)

If I may, I'd like to quote Gore Vidal: "Style is knowing who you are, what you want to say, and not giving a damn."

■ Wendy James (singer)

Proximity to *moi*. Knowing *moi* automatically validates you among the cognoscenti, the fashionistas, the paparazzi and any number of other vaguely foreign-sounding groups. Being stylish begins with loving who you are. For those who have trouble loving who they are, may I suggest loving who I am? Style is all about expressing your inner self, capturing your personal ethos and spending a lot of someone else's money in the process.

■ Miss Piggy (Muppet)

The most important thing is to have your own style. This phrase "in style" has been ruined and overused — you don't want to hear the phrase any more. Anna Wintour has style in her way.

■ Karl Lagerfeld (fashion designer)

I think that physically a good bone structure helps — having high cheekbones and a certain kind of facial expression makes a contribution. Not too much smiling or laughing. I think coolness is stylish. The way you carry yourself, having a straight back — all of that. Otherwise you can be whatever you want to be. There are stylish big ladies, and stylish small ladies, and stylish short and tall ladies, but roughly speaking a certain kind of bony style — not "model" as such — is a good start. I think someone who has real style has the ability to transfer feeling to their clothes. People wearing black veils for months and months or not taking off their boots for six months — that can be so stylish; it is not necessarily about being clean — it is about expressing your feelings.

■ Anita Pallenberg (actress)

You can be stylish and not necessarily chic. I don't think you have to be chic to be stylish; you can be grungy and still have great style.

■ Chloë Sevigny (actress)

CELEBRITY STYLE
Why some have it, and the others don't

Visiting the Queen

Your average slobby, "crappy" dresser is arguably closer to being stylish than celebrities who are so obsessed with how they look that they'll assume a "walk" or a facial expression. You see it all the time. Trying too hard to the point of not being able to smile is not sexy or free and there is no life in just being a clothes-horse. A bit of kid's snot on a cardigan is much more stylish. It's interesting when you see celebrities revealing a cold, undignified, insatiable aspiration that renders any true absorption of culture and inspiration impossible—that's the opposite of stylishness, chic, texture or individuality. There's something painful to behold about seeing consumer culture fill a desperate hole. As everyone knows, you just can't buy style.

There needs to be evidence of imagination, filtering, ideas, the ability to see things sideways: one's own stuff. It's amazing, actually, how removed from this what's held up as "stylish" often is.

KATE MOSS is endlessly fascinating precisely because she is stylish. She seemed to land effortlessly as style queen of the universe, single-handedly propping up fashion as we know it. Yes, she's rich, skinny, famous and beautiful, but, more importantly, she's original. She has a genuine, fun, sweet kookiness that is unpretentious. People want a bit of her looseness, a bit of her style, which is why they copy her. Her ambition seems to be more cultured than a clawing desperation, and you can sense the freedom. Moss evidently has an opinion, an eye and an appreciation. Her unique experience of fashion has been absorbed into a mix of independent inspirations. She must have drunk in images of Riviera, punk, Anita Pallenberg; she can identify brilliant creativity and interpret it in her own way. Her look doesn't come from nowhere—she pulls in her own knowledge and humour. Clothes are used as a language and she has a keen, intelligent sense of the semiotics. Meeting the Queen, she thoughtfully wore royal blue; she understands what's rock 'n' roll. We're just amazed at how long she's sustained the style mojo at such overdrive.

THE SOURCE

That's you, of course. The source of stylishness. Here we explain why you should be confident, as if you're not already, and then we start getting into the nitty-gritty of how to look awe-inspiring. As a nation that has traditionally taken stylishness seriously, France has come up with a few helpful terms. By the end of this chapter, you'll be fluent in all the French you need to know.

Stylishness comes out of the primal soup.

CHEAP DATE READERS SAY

Perhaps the more integrated a person you are, the less you bother about expressing yourself with clothes. Your health and happiness are more important than being stylish.

Choose your statement items carefully.

What are clothes for? Function, tradition, attractiveness, modesty, the deployment of power, and prestige.

Go to art galleries for ideas and read good literature. If you're socially awkward, let your clothes speak for you.

Make a scrapbook of favorite fashion pics or street photos for inspiration.

If you're prone to low self-esteem, you can tap into your other side — the flamboyant side.

Decide what color you're into at the moment. Dance... ballet, modern, tap, swing, flamenco... movement – that's inspiring.

If I think about it, I've had some of my most fun times when I've been wearing something spontaneous and probably inappropriate.

An awareness of twentieth-century history helps — context! Never make fashion a chore or an infringement on your life.

Experiment until you find something that makes you feel good — it doesn't matter what everyone else is wearing.

We're surprised when stylish people are like the rest of us, just better looking and better dressed.

Get passionate about something and then you've immediately got style.

You're never too old to have a "pointless" dressing-up session with your friends.

Body

Rebel against feeling dissatisfied with your body, because it's a ridiculous thing to be. If this book were a step-by-step guide, this would be the first step: when it comes to how you look, focus on the positive, and don't be thinking, "God, my ass is really fat." Everyone has something about themselves they feel is beautiful. No buts (heheh). Ignore "rules" of proportion — that stifles the imagination, though, sure, if you've got a beer belly, then tight hipsters and a short baby tee will be hard to work. Accentuating the asset you love — great hair, amazing boobs, slim ankles, high hips, clear skin, long eyelashes, a winning smile (everyone has one of those), kissable cheeks, good fingernails, languid eyelids or whatever — is strengthening. By not coveting what other women have, there's nothing to feel less than. At the risk of sounding cheesy, our bodies are always worthy of the loving amazement our mothers had for us as babies.

La belle laide

J. M. Barrie wrote of charm, "If you have it, you don't need to have anything else; and if you don't have it, it doesn't matter much what else you have." *La belle laide* is French for "the beautiful ugly"; a woman who is not conventionally attractive but whose allure outshines regular prettiness. Style is charm. It's an underestimated tool of empowerment and a brilliant mechanism for transcending your body complexes, whereas fashion, constant celebrity and ideas of what you "should be" are undermining. Old-fashioned, thought-out "style," like a classic, well-fitting, immaculate pair of tartan pants and neck scarf just so, predates modern ideas of beauty but has its same original power. The concept of "beautiful ugly" is part of the depth of stylishness. Beauty alone limits things somewhat. That's one of the reasons why a gorgeous actress in a fabulous evening gown often lacks style.

10,000 people went to see grandmother Liz Renay streak down Hollywood Boulevard in 1974.

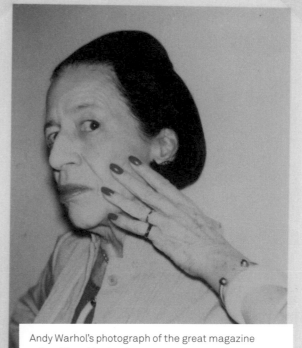

Andy Warhol's photograph of the great magazine editor Diana Vreeland.

Don't be cowed

We are all trying to conform yet simultaneously to individualize ourselves. The horrible feeling of being judged for the way you look, left out or marginalized, is painful for a young person, and frustrating. You know you have something to offer, but you feel ignored because you like to wear pinafore dresses, or go for a '50s preppy skinhead rockabilly casual punk look, or what not. People who get their toughness from being in a gang and having a narrow consensus about how people should look just aren't stylish. Normal, imaginative, sensitive, thoughtful people are the ones striking out and being vulnerable. Style can be the witty riposte to feeling rejected, a battleground or canvas for the struggle and ambition to find one's niche. Mistakes are not just allowed, they're a must.

Cecilia Dean, founder of style bibles *V* and *Visionaire*, escaped small-town America for New York in search of the like-minded, and found them.

"The popular girls back at school were never stylish."

Cecilia Dean

Fashion

Because fashion is unstable, being "in" can be tense and stressful, but there is also a positive, enthusiastic, inspiring flow to changing fashions. They are always new and exciting. And if fashion turns its eye to something you're already into, then the shops will be full of what you like, and in a short time you'll have boosted your collection of stripy tops, gypsy skirts, pixie boots, woven belts, little '60s dresses or big necklaces, and the trend will be forgotten very quickly. Whether you are a bemused observer of fashion, warily absorbing what you like, or taking part in the road show, to be stylish it's important to have, or to try to have, a wider horizon. Beware the insane language of fashion journalism.

Don't believe the magazine page-filler telling you that you have to have it. Celebrity fashion, such as getting the latest "it" bag, puts unrealistic financial pressure on people, and it's not necessarily stylish. Spending a lot of money as a style shortcut will backfire; to need to have it is really falling victim to consumer-culture sickness.

BUY IT! ®

GET THE LOOK!

SURVIVE
ON 20 PAIRS
OF JEANS

3 Easy Steps
To Improve
Your Smile

SURRENDER
YOURSELF TO
THIS SEASON'S
KEY FRIGHTWIGS

SHOES...
TO DIE FOR

PERFECTION

WHAT
TO DO

AUTHORITATIVE,
EXPERT ADVICE
ON YOUR
ESSENTIAL
BUYS

WAR ON:
SOCKS

TRACEY EMIN

Is there a classic "Tracey Emin" item of clothing?

There is always a classic item of clothing, but it varies. Speedo webbed swimming gloves; espadrilles; YSL jackets (before, secondhand; now, new!). And tons of brown natural cleavage.

What's your relationship with fashion?

Up and down. I've a lot of friends in the fashion world. But I'm far more interested in good quality clothing than the idea of being somewhere new. I modelled for Vivienne Westwood — it was in Paris at the Louvre. I went out between Jerry Hall and Alek Wek.

Is trendiness a good, bad or indifferent thing?

It's for young people.

If having style requires self-belief, could you tell us why stylish people often seem to have low self-esteem?

Speak for yourself! No, seriously, a lot of people spend more time and energy on how they look instead of what they are and what they do. It's important to be fit, mentally as well as physically.

Does what you wear help you "be" someone?

Yes. Definitely. It can enhance who you are, but not make who you are.

Do all the commercial messages around you undermine your personal style?

They don't undermine my style. I'm just out of the loop on that one.

What are you inspired by?

Really intelligent conversation, surreal dreams, people who work hard.

What are your style influences?

Men in the City [businessmen], vintage sportswear, international princesses.

Good places to get specific things and why?

For years and years I had to buy secondhand clothes. I had Chanel suits, Dior dresses, and I nearly destroyed my feet by cramming them into stilettos. I have no secrets where I buy my clothes or my shoes. I just relish and enjoy the fact that now I can buy them new.

Practical style tips?

Clean fingernails. Nothing too high-waisted, unless it's totally intentional. Dress appropriately for the occasion. Wear jeans two sizes too big. Roll up tracksuit bottoms. Men's shirts buttoned incorrectly. Always take the stiffening out of collars. Never wear shoes with heels that are four inches or higher for more than three hours, unless you have back-up flats in your bag, a driver or someone who can carry you. Always dress correctly for the season. (Coat in winter.) Always have your bras fitted. If your weight fluctuates, don't just get clothes that fit, make sure your underpants aren't too tight or baggy as well.

> ## "I know my French isn't that good but I could hear them saying: 'What's that troll doing on the runway?'"

Fashions you like?

Classic tailoring, sumptuous ball gowns. But at the moment I want to wear things that are short. I have never shown my legs off, but I'm at the age where you have to make the most of your good parts and hide the rest, and just hope to God when you go out that you don't look like [what we English call] a Benny Hill woman — great from the back!

Your distinct silhouette

Hitting upon a shape, a silhouette that complements your figure, posture and mentality, that's so fantastically "you," even from a distance —this is your style. People who have decided to brand their lovable, distinctive selves also appear to lead charmed existences. This might sound hard, but being definitive can be very subtle and understated, the result of thinking about exactly how you like your pants to taper, the space between the top of your riding boots and the bottom of your skirt, the type of shoulders, collar and cuffs you like, and being understood by your alterer (see page 34). Unsubtle is allowed too —there could be something very cute about someone who wouldn't be seen dead without wearing novelty socks.

Civilized vs. primitive

Style is primitive. It's about real, felt aesthetics, but in practice the way of the slob is the way of the downtrodden, and the role of the dirty and smelly is the outcast. Style isn't necessarily civilized, but having style with effective self-restraint is powerful, and we highly recommend it. A dirty, starving junkie could look stylish, but the brand of style we're more interested in is the "winner" brand, and taking care of yourself is part of it.

French Socialist leader Ségolène Royal is perfectly *soignée*.

Les petits soins

How do we dress the naked body, how do we use it and project it? One of the reasons why French and Italian women look so good and so stylish — because they do; the women, not girls so much — is that they look after themselves: they care about *les petits soins*, the little things. Looking effortlessly groomed, and not plucking yourself to high heaven, shows you value yourself. It's dignified, and then you can get away with more. We remember when hairy 'pits were perfectly acceptable for women. Resist the "feminine ideal" of freakishly plastic celebrities and unnatural beauty regimes. Looking after yourself is more about self-love, and femininity. Beautiful smells, dainty lingerie, a dressing table, a satin dressing gown, moisturized skin — it's personal. Why not have a bed head, hair loosely scrunched up, with your favorite pair of old cords? We're not talking about looking prim and pristine, just *soignée* ("cared for" or "polished'). It's that subtle thing that people might not even notice on a conscious level. Looking *soignée*, finding your own *petits soins*, takes a lot of looking at *moi* in the mirror and having *beaucoup de* fun experimenting, which should be guilt-free.

Hollywood knows a bit of dirt can be sexy.

SOPHIE DAHL

Do you ever just let your appearance slide, just have greasy hair and not care?

No. I try hard not to. I'm very old-fashioned; for me part of the essence of being a woman is about being kempt. Looking and smelling good. I love the routine too; there is something comforting and reassuring about it for me.

You say old-fashioned. Have things changed?

I think they have become more obvious, and I think that takes the mystery and allure out of it all a bit. I don't want to know about people's hair extensions, waxing routines or eyebrow plucking. It should be more mysterious and seemingly effortless. Just go and do it quietly, and not be desperate.

What is your beauty regime?

The classic one: cleanse, tone, moisturize, and then a facial once a month.

What would be your main beauty tip?

Always wash your make-up off before you go to sleep.

How many days in a row do you wear a pair of socks?

Never more than one!

What's your favorite piece of make-up?

Mascara, which I wear during the day — and then at night I add eyeliner.

Would you rather wear an ugly but clean polyester tracksuit or a beautiful but dirty Chanel dress?

The tracksuit!

Does your home have the same sparkle and cleanliness as you do?

Yes. I have a cleaning lady twice a week, and I do it too. I just hate dirt and find cleaning therapeutic — and I love polishing the floor!

I can't remember not being intrigued by beauty rituals. When I was growing up, I was surrounded by my mother, my aunts and my grandmother — all beautiful, glamorous women. I used to watch them at their dressing tables and be fascinated by the ritual of putting on a face for the world.

Your crowning glory

Ieva's hair has a wonderfully whimsical and unfashionable Edwardian vibe. If you have long hair, strong arms and a grip on bobby pins (an enviable skill), pin a bun to the top of your head so that the sides bulge all around. This looks so elegant, sexily accentuating the curve of the nape of your neck.

Have a ready supply of hair accessories. It's quite nice to browse in cheapo drugstores and find hair stuff. Of course, the classic simple band is the best. See more in the Accessories chapter.

Plaits, twists and braids are rarely seen, and look so pretty.

A ponytail quickly made, with wisps that have naturally fallen at the sides (hair needs to be the right length), always looks demure and unaffectedly good, whether you're working, lolling or out for grand, formal events. Hair in bad condition often looks great in a ponytail. Its stiffness can make birdlike, pointy shapes at the ends, and raises the crown naturally.

Watch out for hairdressers who are fixated on mullets (the trendy second-time-round ones). You can usually tell just by looking at them.

A very ornate hairstyle looks brilliant if you "own" it.

A good untrendy haircut and color will set you up, and the rest just falls into place. There's no need to pore over every strand. Scruffy hair is sexy.

Makeup

Men don't tend to wear makeup, so why should women? No reason… except that we can! It's there to make you more beautiful, and if the mood takes you, to follow through a "vibe"— black eyes with a '60s dress, for instance. We're not suggesting you always wear makeup, but here are a few tips:

Illustrator Daisy de Villeneuve shows how a brightly colored lipstick or eyeshadow can be your only accessory.

Tidy eyebrows are a much-underestimated way to lift the whole face and give it a cleaner shape. Wipe gently with toner after plucking and don't overdo it, just neaten — unless you have trademark eyebrows.

Instead of eyeliner, why not use a very fine brush with dark eyeshadow? It's more smoky.

Top celeb makeup artist Charlotte Tilbury says: "Apply about five layers of mascara. All the way to both ends, so it's on super thick — this will give you that '60s/'70s kitten look. Very sexy. The boys love it, although of course they don't know why."

Actress Emma Malin goes the extra mile: striking, beautifully done makeup with a slouchy outfit can look brilliant.

Lips don't have to look "bee-stung" to be attractive.

MISCHA BARTON

More than ever, it seems actresses get press coverage just for being "stylish." What do you think?

Yes, there's a lot more media attention on actresses and their style now and the strange thing is, they decide if you are stylish. I rarely agree with their decisions. My "style" is always changing, it's never been constant. You can become famous for a second in a second, and be thrust into the spotlight. It's not about your acting. They just think that you're stylish… or not…

Are clothes an outlet for your self-expression?

They are the personality on your body? I never understood that. People ask me what is my style; I say eclectic. One day I feel rock 'n' roll, the next I feel hippie. My style life goes through stages. For a long time I was into the laid-back '60s and '70s vibe. There are so many things I want to be. One minute a 1930s Dietrich heroine, the next a Cecil Beaton girl; I wanted that look for a long time — really pale with red lips and too much jewelry. It didn't suit me, but you try everything once! Well, I do…

What do you think of the Hollywood stylists?

If people are always styling you, you can become fashionable and you can get a certain confidence but it's always a little bit more forced coming from that direction. It's not a real extension of you — somebody's putting upon you. Many young people are afraid of being true to their own style. LA is a blending kind of place — there is a vibe out there to have to look hot, trendy, of the moment, and very Hollywood — people get sucked into that, and they look uncool and unfashionable, because of course the result is that they end up looking like everyone else. People just copy without a single thought for themselves.

Marianne Faithfull

Le British Punkeroos.

What are you into at the moment?

On one hand I'm into that ethereal kind of look. I love embellished things, but the flipside is almost my favorite look: the plainer and simpler, the better. I don't think there is anything sexier on a woman than a pair of jeans and a big white T-shirt. And jewelry. So sexy. It's not about it looking flattering or making you look thin… it just looks so great. Nothing sexier than laid-back style. I love things being mismatched. A Chanel-chain-bag-with-shitty-clothes look. That's why I love Chanel — it's always classy and classic. They lent me my prom dress. I love the whole thing of pretty, but not, you know what I mean? You can so play with that with Chanel.

How important to you is it that something fits?

When I buy things I don't try them on. If I love something I just buy it. It just doesn't occur to me to get things altered. I don't care if it doesn't fit perfectly, if it's the idea that I want to feel, then that is enough for me.

Do you think style can be acquired?

It's not that important in a lot of people's lives. But I do think that clothes are a born passion.

Cecil Beaton's eye for color and the refined passion for fashion that comes across in his books is a rich source of inspiration.

Who were you inspired by when you were growing up?

I was really into the whole English punk thing; it was my way of rebelling when I was growing up in the USA. I reacted much more to pictures of English girls than to American women; Marianne Faithfull I just related to and I always had a picture of her on my wall. I felt I knew where she was coming from. I loved her style; particularly that pretty biker look that she did so well. Tough but pretty. When I looked at pictures of Marianne I would feel more like her than, say, Marilyn Monroe. I didn't want to be glamorous and sexy. I wanted to be cool in the true meaning when the word was invented — suave, glamorous, cool! Effortlessly cool. I think I fell in love with the '70s from looking at images of my mother in the late '60s and early '70s. I look exactly like she did when she was my age. Her style was so individual. She seemed so '70s London to me. She was the reason I became interested in fashion, utterly inspiring to me in every sense. She was never conventional. I wish she'd saved some of her wonderful clothes!

Are you into accessories?

I love them, although I only wear jewelry that's meaningful to me. I'd love to wear more, but it really has to mean more to me than just decoration. I love bags; I'm obsessive about them.

Underwear

We don't want to bang on about it, because there isn't much to say apart from the obvious: well-fitting underwear is a crucial part of the whole "being stylish" deal. Coco Chanel always said it's good to look as if you're naked under your clothes, and we agree with her, 'coz Chanel woz stylish. Good underwear helps create a smooth line, whether that line is narrow, or round and curvy. The right-fitting bra makes your breasts look bigger. So let's put on some clothes.

Oops! Caught on camera.

Paris and Nicky Hilton getting ready.

THE BASICS

Wake up, throw anything on; look and feel great without thinking. Wouldn't it be heavenly? If you have a good-quality basic wardrobe of simple, timeless, practical, interchangeable designs, that fit you, then you're living sweet. Even with eyes glued together with sleep, you can't miss. Buying "basics" is just part of the flow of need, but they're worth thinking about for a second.

Debbie Harry keeping her basics simple, though rolling your sleeves up might be a good plan.

Keep basics simple, then you have a foundation to build on. Go to the unsullied source of your inspiration where you can, avoiding anything reworked and subverted as part of a trend. This can mean research — if you happen to like the style of Georgian dancing boots, perhaps someone at the Georgian embassy knows where you can find the real thing.

FASHION DETAIL IS STYLE DEATH

Jeans that are prefaded, predistressed, patched or torn, with "fashion"-cut pockets and stitching — no! Unless you insist. You can make anything yours. But know that fashion detail usually makes people look unmysterious. We're saying a white shirt should always just be the classic white shirt, pulled together and chic. Same goes for it all, jeans, suit or T-shirt. Basics are easy because basic is chic and they give you so much scope for being stylish that you can hardly go wrong.

Lauren Hutton, queen of less is more, demonstrates this ethos perfectly.

Uniforms and professional clothing can make great basics, like these scrubs from *www.allheart.com*

BASICALLY...

Soft, natural fibers

Cotton, new wool, silk, angora, cashmere and linen feel good — to yourself and others. They hang better, wear in better, last longer, and they're still the warmest, coolest, lightest, softest, and most breathable. As long as someone is aware that synthetics look trashy and can play with that, then fine, but that's quite a specific look. Beware of the hideous shine that cotton-and-Lycra-mix tops and tights can have. Not a good look. There are exceptions. A tiny bit of stretch in denim has refreshed the staple status of jeans — helping us achieve that '70s super-tight fit without severe "private" discomfort.

Unisex: An extremely cool word

Tops just look better when they're a bit loose. It's good to remind ourselves that it's cooler not to expose every contour. Surfin' the curves, innocently hinting at what's underneath, is chic and sexy; the "packaging" looks less intentional.

Funnily enough, unisex swings both ways. Men can look unbelievably sexy in women's clothes. Think '70s Rolling Stones. Or is that just us? Hmm.

Take a man's T-shirt, especially one that's a little battered after a few turns in the washing machine with lots of softener, and add a pretty brooch.

The boyfriend's shirt, not quite stolen, is a staple, or trophy, for some. With cut-off (men's) jeans, sneakers, tanned legs and a straw hat turned askew. Irresistible.

Establishment is the new anti-establishment. Women rarely venture into the old-fashioned world of gentlemen's tailoring. Nor do men, for that matter. Tap into an enormous wealth of tradition and knowledge with a bespoke chalk-stripe suit, shirt and shoes, and discover a different level of authority. Not cheap, but over a lifetime, a bargain, and, believe it or not, you'd be indulging in a bit of antidisestablishmentarianism.

SURFIN' THE CURVES IS CHIC AND SEXY

Sexiness is not as simple as just being "feminine."

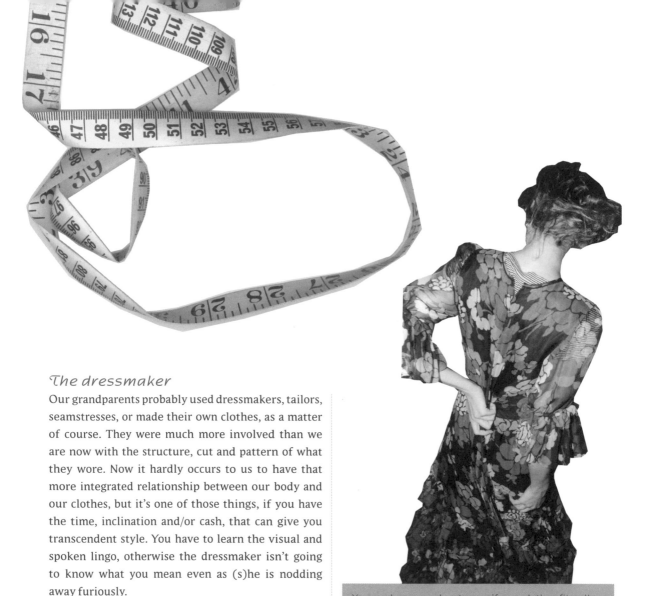

The dressmaker

Our grandparents probably used dressmakers, tailors, seamstresses, or made their own clothes, as a matter of course. They were much more involved than we are now with the structure, cut and pattern of what they wore. Now it hardly occurs to us to have that more integrated relationship between our body and our clothes, but it's one of those things, if you have the time, inclination and/or cash, that can give you transcendent style. You have to learn the visual and spoken lingo, otherwise the dressmaker isn't going to know what you mean even as (s)he is nodding away furiously.

They put women into brackets of size 8, 10, 12, etc.; but what about sizes 9, 11, 13? When I'm making a garment for someone, I take everything into consideration: long arms, for instance, the way a fabric falls on the person, the shape of their body, and try to highlight their best bits. Wide-legged pants, for example, should always be half an inch off the ground. Any higher than that looks a bit clownish.

Gina Izu, dressmaker, who makes entire wardrobes for her clients.

You can be more adventurous if your clothes fit well.

The alterer

Clothes that fit, unless they're meant not to, are plainly the foundation of looking well dressed. Sort out your growing and guilt-inducing sewing pile in a stroke by striking up a platonic if slightly flirtatious relationship with the alterations specialist at your local dry cleaners'. If you're in this habit, a wardrobe of clothes that fit you and you only, with dresses that curve into the small of your back, pants just so and unique buttons is, well, a good thing!

A FEW BASIC SUGGESTIONS

You don't want a comprehensive basic-wardrobe "prescription." Yuck! But here are a few ideas you can't go wrong with. These basic suggestions are interchangeable. Imagine someone walking in wearing black pumps, opaque tights, a big coat and a flowery shift dress — it looks great anywhere. Easy-peasy.

Patti Smith "owns" her cami top.

Drew Barrymore gives hers an optimistic feel.

The dressmaker

Our grandparents probably used dressmakers, tailors, seamstresses, or made their own clothes, as a matter of course. They were much more involved than we are now with the structure, cut and pattern of what they wore. Now it hardly occurs to us to have that

The white tank top

Hard, athletic, action-film heroines Lt. Ripley and Sarah Connor subverted the image of the "wife-beater." It's a definitive, sexy, effortless bit of unisex clothing. You can't get any more basic; somehow, there can't be any more reduction. It needs to be close to 100%-cotton jersey, ribbed or not, with a relaxed fit, sleeveless and with dipping neckline. The plain white tank is intrinsically revealing so it doesn't matter quite how it fits — the nonchalant sexiness it puts across is always arresting and cool.

Twin Peaks' Sherilyn Fenn illustrates how a slim cashmere sweater conjures both innocence and the vixen.

Jackie O in gold hoop earrings.

Basic jewelry

Gold and silver earrings, neck chain, locket, charm and bracelets. Small or large touches of real gold or silver give you magic, take you out of the banal and give you shiny edges. Gold gives you sunshine and valuableness; silver lends a more occulty, moony, gothic image. These could suit daily use:

Gold hoop earrings.

Diamond earring studs. Little sparks of perfection. A very good staple.

Jewelry with personal value is just part of who you are, but even those pieces are worth re-evaluating every few years.

The cashmere sweater

There is something so refined and luxurious about wearing cashmere, for you and for whoever happens to touch you. Cashmere comes from the fleece of goats reared by nomadic Mongolian herdsmen and is usually milled in Scotland. It's a genuinely exotic fabric, and it mixes well with silk.

The greater the ply, the thicker the thread; the greater the gauge, the looser the knit. A little bit serious, cashmere sweaters are preppy, French, universal and super-comfy. You can't have too many, but beware of moths. You can keep good quality, well-maintained cashmere for a lifetime and leave them in your will to your grandchildren.

Plain loose men's sweaters in solid colors make the day happen, with tight corduroy pants and a simple gold chain, locket or necklace.

An almost clichéd basic staple is the dead serious, black, ribbed roll-neck.

Most delicious of all is a fine cashmere sweater dress.

Black opaque tights

They're a foolproof way to make your legs look like pins. They have to be seriously opaque — not even a hint of underpants underneath, so you can wear them with just a top — go on, we dare you! They absolutely have to be matte, like a velvety black hole from which no light escapes. There's no need for high heels, but when they are worn with black suede stilettos the effect is unreal. We're talking 120+ denier here. Ice-skating tights are the ultimate. Wooly tights are really characterful — their dowdiness looks brilliantly incongruent with a short skirt. *www.mytights.com* is a good starting point.

Painter's pants

You can get them at most hardware stores or websites like *www.workinggear.com*, and they are always a great cut. Big and summery, the 100% cotton crumples beautifully. They're the greatest undiscovered secret in fashion. Shhh!

MARY QUANT

You invented tights in the '60s. How?

I had to get manufacturers to make tights because the skirts were so short. Stocking manufacturers didn't want to do that because they didn't have the right machinery. I persuaded somebody to find machinery that could, so the tights could match up with skinny-ribbed sweaters, and other pieces that went together to make up a whole look.

Did you also invent the mini-skirt?

I grew up wanting to move, dance and run — not wearing the clothes I saw "grown-ups" wearing, which were so inhibiting. Nobody told me I had to go to a couture collection and then make a cheap version of what I saw. I just started straight in, designing clothes I wanted, and found that many of my friends and other students wanted them too. Everybody argues as to whether I invented the miniskirt or not, but certainly I didn't see anybody else doing it. London girls had the best legs in the world, or London attracted the best legs, certainly — I think everybody agrees about that! I had a wonderful audience to wear my clothes, and my skirts were the shortest.

Who do you find the most stylish of all?

Elsa Schiaparelli, who did so much, and of course Coco Chanel. Always Chanel.

Ballet flats

So what if they're everywhere? We still love them. What is it about ballet flats that make them so elegant? They suggest innocence, and a body that can move beautifully. The classic shape is perfectly unobtrusive, coolly flat-heeled and smart. We can't think of anything you can't wear ballet flats with. Light-pink-leather real ballet shoes from Gamba or Freed (*www.allaboutdance.com*) look unbelievably sweet fully soled (for about $15) with navy jeans and a plain sweater or T-shirt.

Big, glamorous, comfortable warm coat

If you've just had a baby or if life is taking its swings and roundabouts, as long as you have a beautiful big coat you can throw on, you're living sweet. It's about protection and comfort, on an emotional as well as a practical level. With a lovely big collar to hold up at your neck on windswept days, you're a *femme fatale*, glamorous and mysterious in the aisles of the supermarket. A giant cashmere trench, belted messily like a dressing gown, or an over-the-top, swamping fake fur, its satin lining soothing the unmentionable fashion disaster underneath, these coats tend to cost $4,500 new or a damn sight less secondhand (see *Under the Radar*, page 73), and good fake furs sometimes pop up in chain stores. In the summer, sunglasses perform the same trick.

From left: Kira's father, Gray Jolliffe; our illustrator, Lucie Layers; Marcel Duchamp; and the original *Bionic Woman,* Lindsay Wagner, demonstrate how a fur coat (fake these days is good enough) is glamorous.

Mischa Barton.

Actress Carisa Glucksman.

Jane Fonda. Throw-on dress, throw-on cardigan, tousled hair, steamy.

Jeans

One thing about jeans these days is that the prevailing fashion is all you can find, and its shape is very specific. It's worth trying to find the blankest of shapes that can ride through it all, giving you a wider canvas for more individuality. To be specific, we mean straight-legged jeans with a medium waist height (just below the belly) that suits you. New York is where to go for them: they're half the price and there's a bigger choice of styles—America is where they're from, after all. It's worth buying job lots of your perfect item. Ten pairs of '60s or '70s black or grey Lee cords, 32-inch waist, long leg, please!

The all-occasion throw-on dress

Things haven't changed much in millennia. There is nothing more instant than getting "dressed." You don't need anything else. Any girl could use five of these no-brainers, reliably seductive, wanton yet businesslike, as easy to throw in the wash as they are to throw on. The best of these are but flimsy body coverings, taking the smallest space in your suitcase but making the greatest impact.

The relaxed jersey dress, a vintage '40s tie-back flowery dress, the classic little black dress, the pinafore, the wraparound, the djellaba, the kaftan — fitted, loose, with or without built-in support, the perfect all-occasion throw-on dress is your friend. With bare feet or a pair of simple sandals, or in the winter a pair of black boots and an overcoat, it's just pure sexiness.

IRIS PALMER

Iris Palmer is a painter living in London.

I like jeans that are almost flares but they're not. For someone who hates flares, I have a perverted compulsion to put them on — a kind of Felicity Kendal ['70s British TV housewife] thing, which I've always been drawn to. Like a turtleneck with a shirt over the top. This shape is the compromise. I have to have long jeans; I hate short jeans because I like them to crumple up at the bottom. The shape of the bottom of your jeans is as important as shoes.

I'd love to have a minimal wardrobe with everything high quality, good materials, normal and plain, good cut. I've always admired the French ethos of a good quality, classic, basic wardrobe. Three pairs of drainpipe jeans that fit amazingly, three cashmere turtlenecks, one jacket, ballet flats and that's it for the day. I'm getting there. For parties I have a selection of minidresses. Prudish on top, but just really short. Barely covering my bum.

I'm obsessed with navy blue, because it's got more depth than black. You can look further into it, almost. It's the same as black in the silhouette, but it's got color. Navy blue is the uniform thing as well. If you don't want to make a statement, just want to merge in. Navy is chic. It's understated. Subtle. Anonymous. And less boring than black, less grim. I love navy blue. It suits my coloring.

Now I'm getting back into being experimental. For a long time I just wanted to look formal. This whole thing of being efficient, but the clown is coming back in a subtle way. I'm getting back into color.

The point of this outfit is the silhouette.

GETTING MILEAGE OUT OF YOUR BASICS

Juxtaposing the simplicity of basics with extra touches looks something else. Coco Chanel first did this by wearing masses of costume jewelry with the plainest and most practical of black jersey dresses. But in the same way that some things look great with a little something added, the basic stuff also looks brilliant just, well, basic. There's a certain type of stylishness in striving towards purity and simplicity, like a monk attaining stillness and quiet.

Scrunch up the sleeves.　　Chinos or variations: wide-legged, wide-waisted pale brown cotton pants.

Get clothes dyed or monogrammed.　　Give it a bit of shine. Jeans with a tee and a PVC jacket.

Wear your basics in. Good-quality denim and leather can take a couple of years to acquire that priceless patina.

Roll up the legs.　　Bunch things up with a brooch.　　Change the buttons or linings.

Add a white lace collar and red bow to a black velvet dress.

Coco Chanel

Experiment with the angle of your collar. Here David Bowie looks out of this world.

Liz Taylor as Gloria Wandrous in *Butterfield 8*.

RACHEL WEISZ

What do you think a stylish person's relationship with fashion is?

Style is about a look that is more thrown together, like just taking one beautiful piece and putting it with jeans.

Do you think having style helps an actress's career?

If you have talent, having style will probably up your ante as an actress.

Who and what are your sources of inspiration?

I like how the French dress. I find French women do that thing. I remember a woman I once saw in Paris; she was wearing a Dolce & Gabbana black dress, a stripy wooly scarf, big thick wooly tights, clumpy shoes; she looked absolutely fantastic. Her hair was a bit shaggy — she looked a bit Italian and she could have been English but was just that little bit chic-er. She wasn't grungy, she wasn't wearing it in an obvious way, she didn't look like she tried. That scarf should never have gone with that dress, and yet it all looked great. It was an evening dress and heels in the day. It was femininity and sexiness. I was really inspired.

Is fit important to you?

Cut is really important. The older I get the more I want a really well-cut piece. I don't like things that aren't well cut any more. I think it's really a shape thing — if you are a waif you can wear anything; if you have curves and boobs you need things that are well cut.

Do you like accessories?

I really love hats, but I don't have the guts to wear them except on holiday. I like boyish tweed caps, and hats with big brims. And I love wide-waisted belts.

Do you have a "basic" wardrobe you can describe?

Jeans in blue and jeans in black. Black and brown round-toed leather knee-length boots. Black and white T-shirts. Ribbed turtlenecks in black and white. Pencil skirts. Wide belt in red and black. Pea coat in cream and navy blue. Stripy French sailor top in navy and white. Black pointy stilettos and red open-toe stilettos.

Who do you think has real style?

I have a thing about Elizabeth Taylor in *Butterfield 8* — she's a hooker with a heart. She wears those '50s sexy clothes, kind of trampy, but great. I also loved the way Lauren Hutton and Diane von Furstenberg looked in the '70s — very feminine and sophisticated, yet laid-back.

THE CLASSICS

Like style itself, classics last forever and remain eternal. They're a safe bet.

"FASHION FADES,
ONLY STYLE REMAINS."

Coco Chanel

Make play with the laces on classic Nikes.

Man's Rolex watch on a woman.

The hoodie is a classic, and loaded with a lot of meaning to play with.

Black velvet trouser suit.

Get your classic inspiration from anywhere.

Unfashionable and fantastic.

A good example of classic originals looking better.

White jeans. Whether the influence is from the Clash, ladies-who-lunched in 2002, or the recent high street resurgence, they're weirdly elongating, and cool.

Loose bun, riding boots, crisp white shirt: Princess Anne's riding obsession comes with the bonus of some excellent style.

Fashion has a spotlight on a conveyor belt of classics, with celebrities promoting whatever is the current one. Classics are created by the process of going through these rounds, and each time they're given an extra layer of meaning to be played with. The trick is to wear classics outside the fashion filter, to buy them rarely, and this simply takes knowing what classics are out there.

There are the old classics. Britain seems to produce its sensible share of these. Traditional knits, tweeds, tartans and "countrywear" are still very much part of the English, Scottish and Welsh identities. They make us nostalgic for days when people's clothes were few, handmade or bespoke, strong and adaptable for various activities and kept for years, even lifetimes. British classics deserve a great big nod.

Harris Tweed is hand-woven and dyed in the Outer Hebrides of Scotland. You can tell it's genuine if it has an Orb on the tag.

Jane Russell inspects Harris Tweed at a factory in the Outer Hebrides in the 1940s.

If it's true that one has to dress according to one's mood, what happens when your mood is: "I can't be bothered?" Classics! That's what happens, if you've got them. Then you suddenly look anonymous, elegant, balanced, controlled and beguiling.

A classic is always the model, the archetype. That's why certain garments are tied in with the labels that create them — they can still guarantee a traditional high quality. As with basics, classics have to be classic. Cover versions of old pop tunes or remakes of classic movies are rarely as good as the timeless originals. The root design is the comforting, luxurious point of classics. Deviating from that makes it throwaway; it has to be done with awareness, genius instinct, a mission or luck. Use original classics as a canvas for fun, and undermine their seriousness. Classics are brilliant for carefully manipulating the message you're giving out.

Publicist Lucy Granville.

My riding jacket is a greeny Harris Tweed from the 1950s, made of pure virgin wool, very lengthening for the legs and giving an eccentric silhouette. Let's face it, there aren't many horses around central London, but the fact that it is made of an incredibly hardy, miraculously waterproof weave and has all these great fastening variations makes it a fiercely practical garment and a joy to wear. It's so redolent of country toff-dom that it's fun to wear in the city and challenge people's prejudices.

Cover versions of old pop tunes or remakes of classic movies are rarely as good as the timeless originals.

LADY MARIA-CARMELA HAMBLEDEN

Lady Hambleden grew up in Italy.

The Italians are very strict about quality. Quality in their accessories is very important. I've grown up with that. In that way I'm spoilt. Anything cheap-looking is unwearable for me. It's rare that I go shopping. I have a lot of old things and I sort of recycle them in a completely different way.

I never throw anything with a good color away. I improvise, mixing different things together, trying things out. People notice. Something old can be an innovation. Sometimes the oddest things hit the right note. Color is important in my life. I enjoy being bold.

With style one has to keep one's place. I'm getting on, and so I find one has to be conscious of not looking ridiculous. I am now really rooted in classics. That's where quality is important. With classics you can't go wrong, and I can be daring in my own way.

Now in fashion you see outrageous things, you don't see well-designed classics any more. It's like the newspapers only printing the bad news. The British want to wear something for a season then throw it out. "Who cares, it's pretty, I like it, I'll wear it for three months then it goes in the dustbin." I was brought up that you buy clothes and then you wear them and wear them and wear them.

SOME OF OUR FAVORITE CLASSICS

The black leather biker jacket

Such an unbelievable classic. It is very, very, very, very cool indeed, even on a man with a paunch. The black leather biker jacket is extremely macho, and begs the question, "Is that woman borrowing her boyfriend's jacket, or is she actually really tough?" It says: "Don't mess with me," though before long it'll have another fashion moment and start saying, "I'm a bit of a sheep." Never fear — this will pass, of course, and the biker jacket's style element will remain. Brando, Motörhead, The Ramones, gay clones, The Sex Pistols and The Clash, they are *essence de rebelle*. A motorcycle is handy for the look, but not mandatory. Black leather biker

jackets pretty much have to be secondhand, in tough leather, with lots of zips and customized with mean-looking studs. Oversized is good with tight jeans or a miniskirt; undersized is figure-flattering and works with a delicate flowery dress.

Ribbed tan tights. Laura turns frumpy sexy.

Tan hosiery

Wearing tan tights in summer, they look like your legs, but strangely perfect. Long leg-hair flattened underneath is certainly a look, but perhaps not a desirable one. A ribbed version (pictured) is warm in winter and adds texture. Musician Wendy James says, "Drugstore hosiery without the spandex shine is very chic and far more sexy than the expensive kind. After a late night, a run up that hosiery is just perfect."

Isabella Rosselini. Perfectly shaped and sized studs.

Grey sweatpants

Grey sweats are the ultimate in slouching-around comfort, far too slobby for life-pivoting job interviews. Yet when you're looking clean, fresh and healthy, they brim with unassuming chic. These are easy classics to play with.

Why not wear grey sweatpants with a pair of high heels?

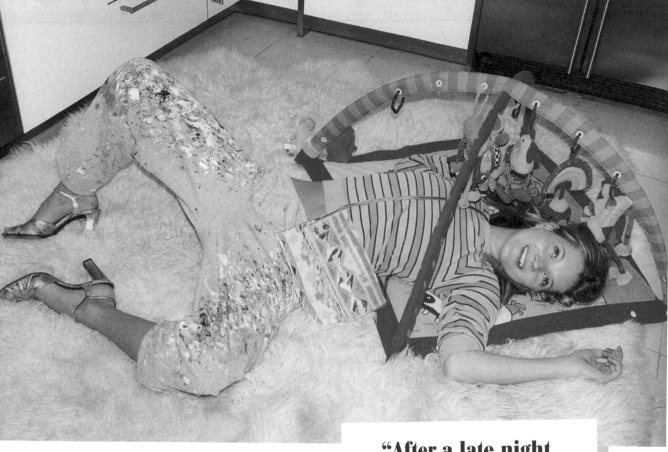

"After a late night, a run up that hosiery is just perfect."

Wendy James

Simplicity itself for under a tenner, these shoes have a great shape.

Kung Fu shoes

Pad silently through life like that style god Bruce Lee, ready to crunch underfoot, with a high-pitched squeak, the bones of anyone who crosses you. Classic black canvas Chinese shoes cost less than ten bucks. Thread the strap through the buckle twice to keep them on.

Laura San Giacomo in *sex, lies and videotape*. Cowboy boots look great with brown legs and a miniskirt.

Cowboy boots

Now so removed from their original use they are more likely to conjure up Rosanna Arquette than herding cattle on horseback. They have to be either the real thing, or the showy-Country-and-Western-lady version — now also a classic.

Wallis Simpson wasn't so much a fashion leader, so much as someone who just looked amazing...

I think it was her wit. She was very severe in the way that she thought. Her wit was razor sharp and her clothes were razor sharp. I read that when she went shopping she had to take chicken sandwiches, in case she got hungry, because she ordered so many clothes.

What do you think stylishness achieves?

Sex... A husband. Admiration. Self-esteem. Confidence. Fun. You can have so much fun playing with bits of jewelry. It's fun to look at someone looking good.

Does what you wear help you be someone?

Oh yes, I step into the part. Actressing, a different part every day. I choose what I wear depending on events or my mood. I hide behind my hat, that's what I want. That's what they're there for. A veil. I can't think of anything better than being veiled. I would have liked to have lived in the fifteenth century, a woman really in charge of her castle. And perhaps you'd have to take in a lover for the night. What's that fantastic film? *La Reine Margot.* That's my ideal. Isn't she incredible?

ISABELLA BLOW

Remembered for her striking hats, immaculate dressing, and her generous, nurturing spirit, Issie Blow understood old-school style. She buoyed the creativity of fashion with her fantastically anachronistic, subversive, and sweet character.

The King of England abdicated to marry Wallis Simpson. She devoted the rest of her life to looking better than anyone else in the room, so he could be proud.

Ray-Bans

Wayfarers: black, plastic and heavy, almost like Bakelite. They harken back to the cool, jazzy 1950s, then to the not-so-cool brat-pack '80s, but who cares? Aside from the current trend, you can make them a staple over a lifetime, so perfect is their shape.

Anything

Anything can be a classic of sorts if you're good at giving things iconic (or ironic) meaning. It's a good way of thinking, as it gives your clothes rationale and roots, and playing with your personal classics communicates your world. What's Ramona (below) channelling with her tracksuit jacket? Here in England, it could be hip-hop, East End geezers, or comedy sketches about Liverpudlians.

With a mini kilt it's perhaps better to go against tradition and wear underpants.

Mini kilt

Girlish, punk, the best tartans have a red background. We advise toning down that whole Japanese Harajuku schoolgirl thing and giving it a bit of sophistication. The tartan mini-kilt's good in winter with a black ribbed turtleneck, black wooly tights and biker boots. This works for a colorful Gujarati-mirrored skirt too.

I like Casuals and '80s hip-hop. When I was younger I was into Grandmaster Flash and that kind of thing. I was a Modette, so Casuals was like a continuation of that. I had a bob, then I started to wear Pierre Cardin tops and stuff. There's something I like about graphic clothes. What I'm wearing relates to the music, I'm saying, "This is what I like." My shorts move it on to the year we're at now. Not actually being '80s hip-hop retro, just making a nod, I'm mix and matching.

Stylist Ramona Rainey makes the tracksuit jacket a classic; talking serious semiotics and looking seriously cool.

Beth's beret is the perfect cherry to top the cake.

When two classics meet.

The beret

Invented by Basque peasants, this brimless wool felt cap has been adopted by many a chic figure, becoming ridiculously rich with references: armywear; stereotypical old Frenchmen; 1920s film directors; 1950s schoolgirls; beatniks, renegades. The secret of the beret's success lies in its versatility — and that it's universally flattering. Working out your signature version will take a bout in front of the mirror. What look suits you? Forward, back, or cocked? Pulled-down or perched? When you find your perfect balance, rejoice. With Che Guevara, Faye Dunaway, and George Clinton, you have tamed the beret. Classic.

Black Capri pants

Black Capri pants — side-zipping and in a stretch cotton, tight all the way down to the lower calf — are such a chic classic they're almost a parody. The chains have yet to get these right. You need a French catalogue like *La Redoute*. Or do an Audrey Hepburn and take a trip to La Parisienne, Piazza Umberto, Capri (tel. 00.39.081.837.02.83), where they'll take a day to make a pair measured to your shape.

Chanel handbag

The prohibitively expensive Chanel handbag is an icon of iconicness. It inhabits that special place where a cheap emulation of its gold chain is somehow OK. It's to do with the idea that Coco Chanel pretty much invented style as we know it, so to an extent we can lean on her by-products. In fact, in terms of the message you're giving out, a fake Chanel handbag is more comparable with it than a $1600 Fendi bag with knobs on. If you want to shell out on the real thing, a Chanel handbag gives you the freedom to be more scruffy and freaky. The best way to wear the real or fake is with unglitzy clothes: using the brand in a clever way as a statement of attitude. A comfy grey or black hoody, reminiscent of Rocky and '70s joggers and in need of saving from its petty-criminal reputation, is set off wonderfully by that fat gold chain over the shoulder.

MORE CHEAP DATE CLASSICS

Tailored black miniskirt   A message on your back   Very long fitted tweed coat à la *Withnail and I*

Stripes with flowers (a furnishing classic)   White nubuck shoes   Keds   Yasser Arafat scarf

Barbour for real, not overpriced, countryside clothes   Oxford shirt — Brooks Brothers is good for these

Cutoff jeans   Bowling shirts   Swing coat   A silk shirt with jeans, over or under layers, collar out

Djellaba   Hawaiian shirts   Abercrombie and Fitch for basics   Stripy pajamas   Clutch bag

Burgundy waffle cardigans   Army surplus cargo pants   Matching bag and shoes   Ben Sherman shirts

Dr. Marten's work boots   Capezio jazz dance shoes   Capped Oxford shoes   Cartier watch   Flip-flops

Black suede men's Gucci loafers   Hermès scarf and Birkin bag   Black patent belt with patent buckle

Diamonds   Straw bag   Penny loafers   Byzantine peacock earrings   Bright red toenails

Chanel for her ideas — big jewelry, cap-toe shoes in contrasting colors, black velvet hair ribbons

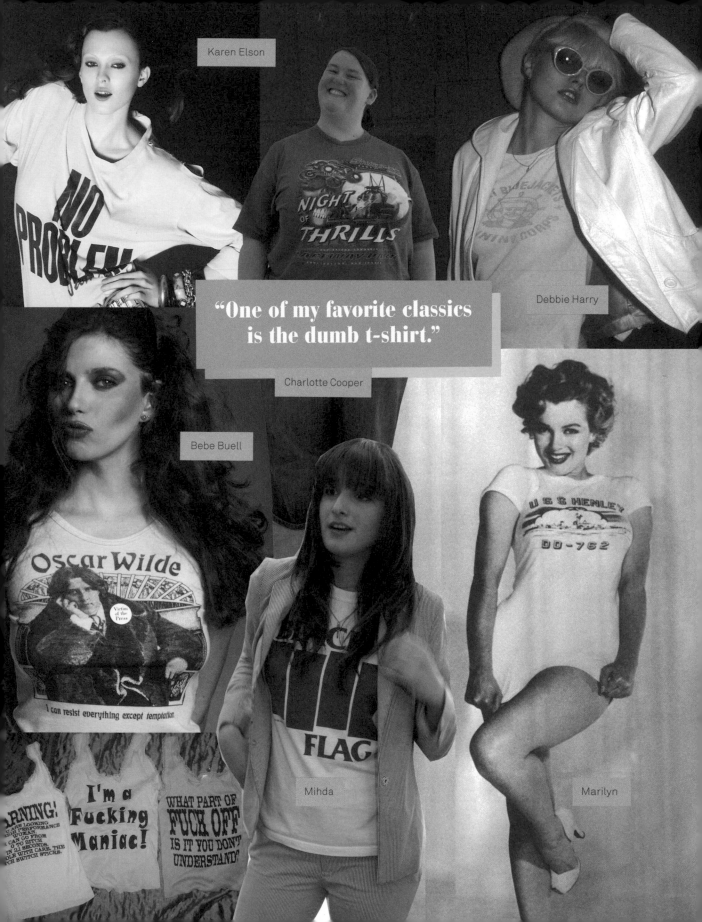

Karen Elson

Debbie Harry

"One of my favorite classics
is the dumb t-shirt."

Charlotte Cooper

Bebe Buell

Mihda

Marilyn

Der Kaiser... and the King.

Is there such a thing as good taste nowadays?

Good taste only tastes good to the people who think they have good taste; good taste can be very uncreative and boring. Good taste is something very bourgeois, very established, so it needs fresh air. People we consider to have bad taste are happy with their bad taste. It's not our problem. It's pretentious to think one is an arbiter of taste. Who cares? What counts is how happy people are with their own garbage. They may think what we have is horrible, no?

Where do you like to go shopping?

I don't shop that often, and I don't go to too many places. I like shopping in book stores. I like to go to antique jewelry shops, to my shirt-maker and to the Dior men's shop. Sometimes I go to Colette just to have a look. When I go, I shop a lot.

What do you think of Elvis Presley's style?

A genuis forever. There's no one like him. The whole attitude.

> "GOOD TASTE ONLY TASTES GOOD TO THE PEOPLE WHO THINK THEY HAVE GOOD TASTE."

If you had invented an item of clothing, what would it be?

The white shirt. Not jeans. I love the white shirt. All my shirts have been made for me since I was sixteen.

Do you think it's important to be well groomed?

I hate people who don't wash. If you're outside slobby, then you're inside slobby too.

Do you think there's anything a woman shouldn't wear?

It depends how they are. Clothes should be right for their look, their lives, their lovers, their children. It has to match something. The Barbie look in the kitchen with three children is grotesque, but play the Barbie in another arena if you have to. I think that overpushed femininity is the most ageing effect in life.

Do you feel that the clothes you design are creations or products?

I like things to be worn, so they are products. There is nothing bad about products. People thinking they are making art, it is a little overdone. Cartier jewelry — that is a product too. I hate the idea that if people think something is a product then it's no good. There can be good products or horrible products. Sometimes the bad ones are even more expensive than the good ones.

Do you think consumerism has become an art?

No, shopping is a cultural activity. Why do all these people want to be artists? I hate nothing more than the cliché of designers wanting to be artists and the fact that the art world hates the idea that fashion people could be artists. Where does art start? There is a bunch of bad artists, and there is a bunch of bad designers. There are good designers and great artists, but who can say this is art, and this not art? Ninety-nine per cent of what people paint is not great art either. So who is the arbiter of the art world? Look at the galleries you see around the city. There is a lot of bullshit in them.

Interview with Bay Garnett first published in British *Vogue*.

Who or what inspires you?

Everything. Inspiration comes from having open eyes.

You have lived in the most refined areas of style, yet you can produce fashion that people love. How?

Chanel is different from what it used to be. It is a label, and people like labels — it is a guarantee. There is a spirit of modernity, and it has to be updated all the time — that's my job. Chanel is about life, and not being boring and commercial. It is about a chic, bright and modern attitude for daily life. There are hardly any clothes by Chanel left from the '20s and '30s, because they were worn so much they were thrown away, or given to the maid. It meant they got used. It is the best thing that can happen to a dress. Runway masturbation — clothes that go to the museum without being worn — I am very much against.

Karl with Karen Elson.

Lagerfeld started designing at the house of Chanel in 1980, nine years after Gabrielle "Coco" Chanel's death (she worked until the very end). He revitalized her trademarks: the handbag, the capped shoes, trims, piled-on pearls and suits.

INSPIRATION

Stuff that gets our juices going.

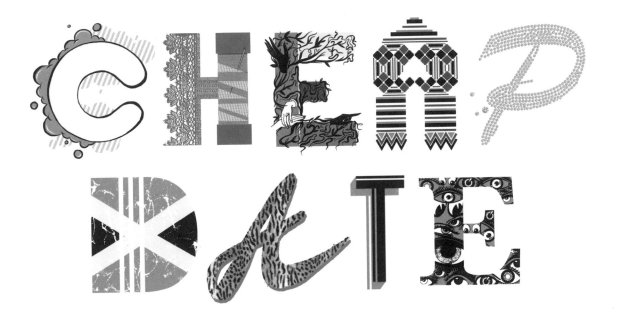

CUTE & KISSABLE

Polka dots & stripes

Convicts in the USA still wear them.

Musician Yadira Grant is distilled cute and kissable.

Fender Stratocaster of the great blues guitarist, Buddy Guy.

'80s duo Strawberry Switchblade lived in a polka-dot parallel universe.

Nancy Sinatra

HABERDASHERY

Lace

Delicacy, femininity, eighteenth-century men, the way Heavy Metal and Goth subverted it, lingerie, pornography, collars and cuffs, Victorian children, frou-frou, nighties, confectionery, trim on anything from shoes to waist to cuffs to collar to hair. Stitched behind and below the hem of a skirt.

Trimmings

Gold metallic bullion fringe is beautiful if not used in the costumey military context. In the hair, wrapped round the wrist, as a sunglasses rope, etc. Just mind you don't look like a pair of curtains. Furniture trimmings when sewn into clothes stiffen them, so if stitched round and near the bottom of your skirt they can give it a nice shape.

The miracle of the safety pin

Invented in 1848 by American mechanic Walter Hunt after fiddling with a piece of wire for a couple of hours.

Use little gold safety pins as stitching on your hem or even seams. If done neatly, the tiny, evenly spaced bits of gold showing through can look posh.

For oversized shoulders – ruche them up with a safety pin. Simple as that – it works well.

Gather your oversized dress into two sets of neat pleats at the front or one set at the back, depending on where the zip is and what look you want. Put a belt over the top and now you look unique.

With three safety pins, a large enough piece of material and much improvisation, make a skirt, top, dress or hat. For extra sophistication, use scissors.

Stick one through your lip. Go on.

ENCHANTING COMPANY

GEORGE MELLY

Lovingly remembered as a jazz musician, surrealist, fishing enthusiast, author, journalist, wit, and thinker, George Melly was incredibly fun to hang out with.

Smart surrealists Louis Aragon, André Breton and Paul Eluard with Elsa Triolet Aragon and Nusch Eluard.

The Royal family, I don't think they have any style at all.

Don't you? We're wondering if the Queen does. She wears such lovely bright colors. She's always very color-coordinated.

I think the Queen is the only one who's bearable, because she does a boring job, very boringly, and that's what she's for. The rest are either young upper-class yobbos or nonentities. The Queen never passes an opinion, and that's what you want, really. The Queen Mother I adored. For a start, she wasn't a member of the royal family — she was a Scottish upper-class woman. She had style, all right. Did she not? And she overspent all the time, and she drank all the time. And she could be very funny. Dalí had style. Some children have style. Drunks can be stylish. Talking of which — cheers!

You're into surrealism.

If you're into surrealism you just have to look sideways at everything. If you have a surrealist training, you see things from a surrealist point of view.

Do you think the way you dress is kind of sideways?

No. The surrealists were very smart, you know. They dressed like bankers, most of them, apart from Dalí. They had their hair parted, their shoes shined, because they wanted to appall the bourgeoisie. And the bourgeoisie fully accepted Bohemianism, so they were very anti-Bohemia.

You described, in *Revolt into Style* [Melly's analysis of the birth of pop music], how the establishment and money-makers absorb sub-cultures.

Yes, there is money to be made, of course. The punk people resisted for a long time. Wouldn't have any part of it. And their clothes were designed by this extraordinary woman.

Vivienne Westwood?

Yes. What a strange woman!

TTITUDES

NANA OFORIATTA–AYIM

Nana Oforiatta-Ayim is a writer from Ghana.

In Ghana we have the traditional dress, which is mainly what the older people wear, and what you have to wear at functions and formal events. The woven cloths will all have some symbolic meaning. They're quite far out. We have this language of symbols. One symbol will be a whole proverb in itself. The colors in the fabric are symbolic too. Red is the color of the earth, of female and fertility; black the color for air or breath, power and time; and white stands for water, for male, and also for purity. Every color symbolizes something and when they're combined they mean different things. People in Ghana are very spiritual.

There are definitely certain ways that you have to dress. It's within a structure that you can't really step out of that much. There's a feeling of belonging. And if you stand out, people will tell you to get back into the norm. People stretch it within the structures — there are a million varieties. It's amazingly creative.

People are very put together. Every girl or woman, however rich or poor she is, goes to the hairdresser's every weekend — every one. It's all about being really neat. People go and have manicures and pedicures. It's not like "messy chic." That's not understood or appreciated at all. On every corner there are about ten seamstresses, because everyone has their clothes made.

You have to respect the people, especially the older people. It's such a culture of respecting. Dressing seductively is frowned upon.

PARIS HILTON

Quite separately from what she does or doesn't stand for, Paris looks like no one else. She's incredible. Talk about having your own style. That's inspiring. Far into the future, her name will live on to describe a look.

"In the late '90s I got some photographs of this girl and her sister. It happened to be the daughters of a hotelier and they were very bourgeois and loved fashion and they were all about money and, you know, they were the Hilton sisters. They were super-intriguing at the time. The sort of antithesis of the '90s, which was more about anti-class. Suddenly, in the late '90s, they brought this ironic, weird, perfect debutante, this bourgeois thing of embracing the establishment. But then suddenly Bush comes in. Like, wow. Hold on… But…people really are buying into this!"

Camilla Nickerson, fashion director, *W* magazine

BELLA FREUD

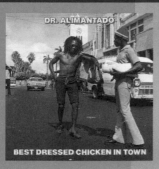

DR. ALIMANTADO

BEST DRESSED CHICKEN IN TOWN

The sportswear look from Jamaica is the best look — like Bob Marley. That track pant with jean jacket, and a hat — very narrow and elegant.

I love Jamaican style. It's that glam thing done with very little. I spent time in the West Indies in my teens. Boys would customize their clothes. They had no money; they really did create an identity with very little. They famously used to customize their outfits in prisons.

There's a record cover I love that brilliantly illustrates the kind of attitude that is the cool, Jamaican style — "Best Dressed Chicken in Town" — the guy is wearing a pair of denim cut-offs and these red underpants. He loves his pants. He is proud of them. He shows them off: really peacock.

Guys will wear Prince of Wales jackets [shooting jackets in a check print invented by the Duke of Windsor before he became Prince of Wales] with nothing underneath. It looks very glamorous, although it is very little. They don't fret about not having shoes and a tie — they wear what they have with such panache and style. Incredible, vain boys doing what they do with the clothes available.

Sunday school is the other Jamaican look I love. Very chic with very little: a little suit with a hat — '60s/Victorian kind of look. The women would wear these little pastel suits and they just looked amazing; very like the president's wife, kind and ladylike and tennis club but always with that bit of raunch.

With Jamaican style there is always a bit of establishment mixed up in it and that is what makes it so irreverent: a bit of Prince of Wales and pinstripe. Something tailored with track pants or army pants. Mixing things that meant something socially.

IN'T ROCK 'N' ROLL GOOD?

The rock 'n' roll look is a '70s thing. It's raunchy, it's about attitude, or cock, ahem, or cockiness. It appears to have something to do with heroin, and libertarianism.

Keith Richards spawned it: the open shirt, the long hair, the scarf, booties or cowboy boots, the vest, the tight leather pants, the skull ring, the accoutrements; flouncy and beastly at once. Where did he get it from? Trying on Anita Pallenberg's clothes is where (see interview with Ms Pallenberg, page 120). Perhaps a bit of pirate, Little Richard and Elvis too.

Iggy Pop was leader of the leopard rock 'n' roll thing, subverting trashy Hollywood glamour.

Johnny Thunders was a kid from Queens in Studio 54–era, anything-goes New York. From boy-scout shirts to Tibetan boots, '40s women's heels to fine tailoring. With a curled lip, he made the slightest detail significant, and magnificent. Mundanity didn't exist in his style, and pictures of him are still magical.

It being mainly a male thing, women got the "groupie" look, which is different — involving feather boas, old floral dresses and red platform sandals. However, Patti Smith, Chrissie Hynde, Joan Jett and Tina Turner all did that rock 'n' roll thing brilliantly.

What we call rock 'n' roll now isn't quite the Keith uniform, much as punk isn't necessarily piercings or mohicans.

Keith Richards

Johnny Thunders

I love Rock-n-Roll

How to look rock 'n' roll

Appreciate Chuck Berry.

Cross-dressing of every sort (gender, class, race, etc.). This is how rock 'n' roll differs from plain "rock."

Be a smartass.

Be sufficiently fired up about the power of good, dirty electric guitar sounds to say, "Ow!" and "Shimmy!" on the dance floor.

Include plastic jewelry, feathers, '30s velvet, leopard, leather, lace, scarves with tassels, red PVC, polka dots, silver jewelry with semi-precious stones, patent leather belts, dusky pink or blue drape coats with black velvet collars, pinstripe vests, tight skirts, tight black leather pants, ankle boots, jewelry that pretends to be something — like a spider brooch — as much as possible in what you wear. A top hat, too, if you want to be a dork about it.

Men with rock 'n' roll fantasies should avoid getting a case of the "Le Bons." Symptoms of the disease include expensive square-toed boots and highlighted hair.

What is rock 'n' roll? Is it more than just two guitars, bass and drums?

It's definitely more than that for me. It's more than music, it's a vibe and an energy that either you got it or you don't. If it's not coming from a true place, then it's not real.

Can you define that vibe and energy?

It's real, animalistic, not thought out, very sexual primal energy. It's instinct; it's how you play, how you move, how you look at people; that part that oozes out of you: what do people see when they see you? How do you make them feel?

Is your favorite outfit jeans and sneakers?

It used to be sneakers, but they stopped making the kind of sneakers I wore. Pro Keds. Everybody thinks Converse are the same because they're high tops, but they're not the same. Converse have narrow feet and Pro Keds had a nice round toe.

TWENTIETH-CENTURY HEROINES

Amelia Earhart (1897–1937)

Lee Miller (1907–1977)

I could never decide if it was humor or just perverse rebellion that made her dress the way she did — with a frilly net toilet-seat cover as a hat, trash jewelry mixed with her Cartier ring.

Antony Penrose, her son and biographer.

In 1932 Amelia Earhart became the first woman to complete the dangerous solo flight across the Atlantic. She disappeared in July 1937, somewhere over the Pacific. Always a tomboy who enjoyed daredevil stunts, she designed a lot of her clothes, wearing a crisp white shirt on all her flights.

Before getting into aviation, she was a social worker, nurse and nutritionist. She never shied away from challenging the set gender roles of the time and was intelligently, gently and wisely outspoken, saying, "Courage is the price that Life exacts for granting peace. The soul that knows it not, knows no release from little things."

The aviatrix is symbolized by the brave, pioneering, simple, utilitarian, yet feminine Amelia Earhart.

Photographer, muse, model in New York and Paris in the '20s and '30s, Lee Miller was the first female infantry combat photographer — during World War II.

A sleek blonde bombshell, Miller was in the first overt advertisement for sanitary napkins. She had a passionate affair and an influential artistic association with Man Ray, a hallmark of which is the solarization of photographs. A successful surrealist, portrait and fashion photographer of remarkable wit and social conscience, she took harrowing and poetic images of battle scenes and a devastated Europe.

She starred in Jean Cocteau's first feature film, *Le sang d'un poète*, as a statue. A popular champagne glass was molded in the shape of her breast.

EYES OPEN EVERYWHERE

Including your friends' wardrobes.

VIVIENNE WESTWOOD

People say that you make the rich look poor, and the poor look rich. Where does this idea come from?

Because the clothes have got such character, they also give the impression of a sort of experience — that somebody has actually lived a life in them. They might even look secondhand. I've always really cared about that, because of the way I make the clothes fit on the body. I think the clothes, when you put them on, have a sort of active feeling to them, and it's as if your own body made the shape of them. The clothes look as if you've had them for a long time, that you've had a big experience in them — experiences both rough and tough. We live in this world of television, where people haven't had much in the way of experience. I think there is a certain richness in looking as if you've lived, as if you have done some exciting things, and you are going to do some exciting things next. It gives people a look of control over their lives, and that they are doing something. I would say that is a way of making them look rich. There is this common-pool-of-experience look to it, so the rich sort of come down, and the poor sort of look the same.

Why do you think your clothes appeal to musicians?

Maybe because they are so dynamic, so attractive; they make a good silhouette. I'll tell you another thing: one theme that goes through my clothes is the idea of the hero. The other thing is that you can make yourself look very individual as well. They are great when you move, and they make you look very, very sexy. They make you look larger than life.

Tell us about the clothes you produce.

I'm not locked into an organization where people tell you what to do. I've always been the judge of what I do; I've always been able to build up my technique, and decide whether I like it or not. I have found a way of making clothes that look like couture clothes, but the method in which they are made is a ready-to-wear method; so my cutting and printing methods are the same as those famous couturiers from the past.

Why, and how does that make someone look sexy?

It depends what people find sexy. What I care about is that my clothes make people look heroic, and they make them look important, and I think that is sexy. It's also to do with changing what people are used to looking at. The best example is the corset, something that people hadn't really seen for two hundred years. Things have to have a dynamic to them. It's a question of what you want; you can be really obvious, or you could be like a nun — that too could interest somebody. For example, the Japanese kimono is a very sexy garment. You can find sexy in all clothes, really.

If you could have three paintings in the world on your wall, which ones would you choose?

Impossible to say, but one of them would have to be seventeenth-century Dutch. I also love the Harlequin paintings of Watteau, and Fragonard is incredible. But I think ultimately it would be Titian, maybe that painting of Diana in the National Gallery that's not finished. If someone gave me an Andy Warhol I wouldn't know what to do with it; I would feel a right idiot putting that on my wall. I don't think his work is worth one penny — I think it's total hype.

Tell us about the amazing cardigan with tons of buttons — too many buttons — that you did?

I didn't invent this, but I reintroduced it, and I think it is absolutely fab — the little button-up cardigan. I think that is incredibly sexy. Wear with nothing underneath — it's just great. Wear it with a little shirt underneath. Undo as many buttons as you like. It's great!

What are the qualities you most value in people?

It is skepticism — people able to question received opinions. They can only do that if they have spent a lot of time discovering ideas — it takes a lot of discipline. What I want more than anything from somebody is to really properly talk about things.

What are your favorite books?

Aldous Huxley is really great. George Orwell's *1984* is definitely worth reading — and is very important, as it is a mirror on the world in which we live.

Are you hopeful for the future?

No. Young people are the ones who are the most distracted of all, their heads are going to be filled with nonstop distraction; they are never going to be able to stop and think, read and look. If you have something in your head — it's not so easy for it to be filled with rubbish.

Do you think people should dress up? Make an effort every day?

I think people should really make an effort, I think people should try to look special — not look like everybody else. I would never wear almost everything I see! I hate these awful production-line clothes.

If you had one piece of advice, what would it be?

It would be not to read magazines, not to watch TV, and then you have to do something else instead.

Do you still have an ambition?

I'm always so glad when I learn something about the world I live in. My ambition is that when I die I'm not stupid — to be less stupid than I am now. You could put it another way; I would like to be more wise than I am now. It is a burning need for me to know more. One of the reasons I want to know more is because I don't want to do harm. I want to help in some way.

What is your favorite part of a woman's body?

The face is everything, really. Your body in clothes is all about the face — everything helps to present your face.

VIVIENNE WESTWOOD

Finally, what did you think of The Sex Pistols?

I thought they were absolutely amazing at the time. They really wanted to do something; to change something. That was when I realized that you couldn't, so anybody who pretends to change the world through rock 'n' roll — it can't be done. The Sex Pistols was the most heroic attempt to confront the establishment — but then it just uses you. You can never confront it, you just end up being a marketing tool in the end.

Interview with Bay Garnett first published in *Vogue Nippon*.

UNDER THE RADAR

If stylishness means congruence with yourself and your soul, then thrifting is a way of living that out.

Bay and Kira's Swap Shop.

If the whole world past and present is our dressing-up box, where do we find it? The chains and department stores have some great clothes, but they are promoted to us so well that we need to be more active in sourcing our true inspirations. Chain stores peddle "fast fashion" — they go for a quick turnover and lack enough substance or nourishment to reflect what a nuanced person you are. To be stylish, you need to be into clothes, and if you're into clothes, you're into finding them.

Indian shop

Flea market

Department store

Scrounged

Borrowed

Hand-me-down

Army surplus

Won in a fight

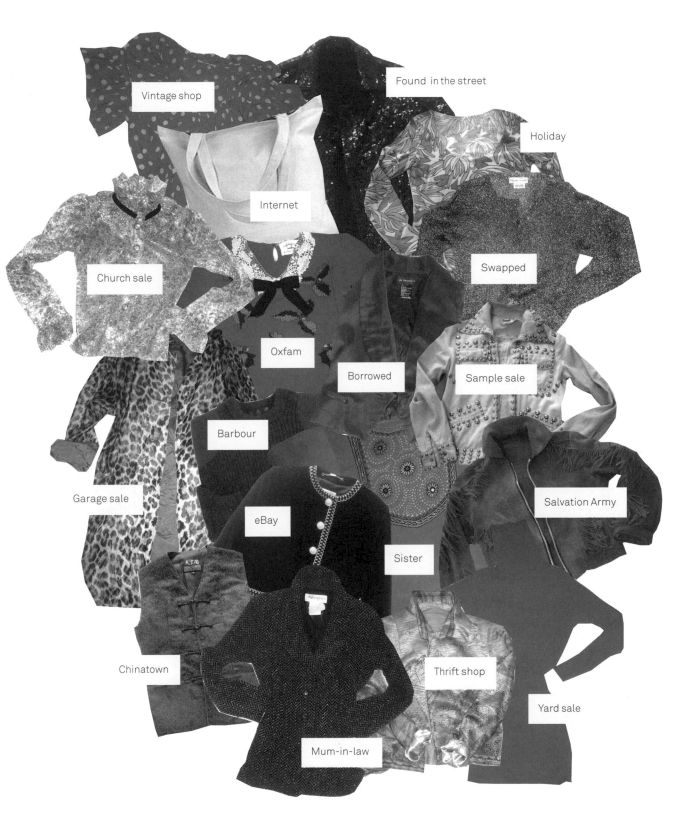

Vintage shop

Found in the street

Holiday

Internet

Church sale

Swapped

Oxfam

Borrowed

Sample sale

Barbour

Garage sale

Salvation Army

eBay

Sister

Chinatown

Thrift shop

Yard sale

Mum-in-law

THRIFTING

We find thrifting infinitely more pleasurable than shopping. It's a relaxed, thrill-of-the-hunt, creative, Bohemian pastime, an archaeological dig, spend-thrifting without too much spending. By going to a yard sale, thrift shops or a market on a lazy Saturday, your wardrobe shapes to you, like a spreading plant. Open up the doors, and sequins, gold, leopard, colorful prints, good tweeds and checks, authentic sumptuous fabrics, a bit of military, lace, pleating, cheesecloth, all unique, invite you in. Going thrifting is about the activity, being outside, rummaging, the community, the feel, the look, the thrill of finding something brilliant unexpectedly: "It's MINE!" A personal, independent pastime, thrifting is labelled as radical, but in fact it is rational and animalistic. Yard sales, church and school fêtes are run by officially the least radical people on the planet, and any stigma attached to the idea of secondhand is irrational.

The chains have tried to absorb "thrifting," which misses the point, and the only result has been to make the word "vintage" vaguely irritating—which we can live with.

IT'S LIKE AN ARCHAEOLOGICAL DIG

Call your friends and have a swap party!

The thrill of the find.

Granny's wardrobe, boyfriends, scavenging, borrowing off friends, swap parties...

You can get a lot of satisfaction from giving clothes to friends you know would love them. Equally, having a reputation for taking on hand-me-downs always reaps rewards. Taking this a step further, organize a swap party in which everyone dumps their castoffs in a big pile on your floor, has a cocktail, then frenziedly attacks the pile. If you want to keep borrowing from your pals, set a strict standard for yourself to concertedly return the clothes, clean and folded, on time.

BETH DITTO

Beth Ditto sings with The Gossip.

This world that we live in makes dysphoria of the body. People can't leave the house because they think they're "too ugly," and get insane plastic surgery. Gee, I wonder why they do that to themselves? The fashion industry makes people feel like total shit. But, at the same time, I really adore some designs. I really wish I could have all these clothes, but none of that stuff would fit me and those designers couldn't give a fuck.

Going to Olympia, WA, from Arkansas was a key part of being eighteen, coming out of the closet, coming to terms with being fat. Realizing there are lots of people just like me there.

I love anything stretchy. Stretch denim is the best thing in the world. I go to shitty shops where you get tank tops with sequins on them, Fashion Gal Plus. Plus meaning it's plus-sized. I want to start a punk-movement line of fat-lady clothes called Elta Berzerk. Weird clothes, all the things I make, with sequins etc.; cut up and safety pinned, multipurpose accessories.

Poly Styrene is my style icon. The very idea that she got braces to look "uglier" — I'm so into her, and the (BBC Arena) documentary *Who is Poly Styrene?* I felt a lot of the things she was going through. Any weak moment, she was "I am not trash. I am who I am."

Poly Styrene of X-Ray Spex.

Local school & church bazaars, rummage sales and yard sales...

Bring on summer, and these fun, community- and family-oriented days out. They are also the cheapest. Discover them in local papers, or just keep your eyes peeled for signs. Find a beautiful old leather music case for $4, a tailored man's suit that fits you for a fiver, or a pair of red-mirrored sunglasses for $1, then have an ice cream. Paradise.

Bay's baby Billy "Bean" Craig is already using his charms to get friendly with the market stall holders.

Markets

Secondhand clothes traders tend to survive on passion and are happy to share it with you. The choice on offer at the really big, established secondhand clothes markets is unmatchable, and your wardrobe will be grinning if you live near one. Paradoxically, because the huge choice is so random, a treasure shines through more visibly. To help that laser eye along, go with your current inspirations in mind. A black leather miniskirt to wear under your favorite big slouchy sweater, a color combination of turquoise and lime green, Diaghilev's Ballets Russes or anything with gold lamé, for instance. It's a neat psychological trick to play on yourself—if you're focusing on something, other treasures can impinge on your peripheral vision, appealing to your unconscious.

With no idea what you'll find, you might have that chance encounter and fall in love with something you've been looking for all your life, perhaps a tight-fitting khaki dress with a big fat brass zip up the front, a '30s panné-velvet scarf, converted during the '60s into a hippie blouse, or the ultimate bomber jacket. You're mainlining inspiration by browsing the original, authentic stuff, and it's because of this that our pet hate is fake secondhand clothes.

Even if you don't buy anything at a big secondhand clothes market, it's interesting to get your eye in. Huge thrift stores in the USA are akin to the choices offered at the Bull Ring in Birmingham or Camden Market in London, and are even cheaper.

JAYNE COUNTY

Jayne County (waving, front), partying in Max's Kansas City, 1974. Spot the other music legends.

By being the original transgendered punk on her arrival in New York from Georgia in the early '70s, Wayne County, who has since permanently become Jayne, has had an untold influence on outrageous, be-who-you-want style.

How did you look back in the '70s?

We were weird-looking, me and this drag-queen friend of mine called Davina Daisy, who looked like Liz Taylor. We would comb our hair and puff it up, and wear eye makeup. We would wear men's pants and loafers, or a man's shirt and high heels. We would take elements of both the male and the female and put them together. That's what shamans and American Indians used to do, but still us street queens were kooky-looking to a lot of the rednecks.

Was it threatening?

It made us a moving target.

Whose style do you admire?

I idolize the old stars. Dietrich, Garbo, Jean Harlow — oohhh, she was beautiful. Another favorite is Susan Hayward.

What do you collect?

Shell jewelry. I love shells. And Egyptian stuff.

Do you have a style tip?

My major fashion tip is how to use pantyhose. Turn the pantyhose upside down, cut out the crotch, cut out the feet and then decorate. Use anything. Glitter, paint, whatever. Then pull them over your head, and you have the most amazing top. I gave that idea to The New York Dolls, and I still wear pantyhose tops myself. I love the idea of taking something that is made for one thing and using it for something else.

Do you have a beauty regime?

I do actually. I have a little glass of wine before I start to get ready.

Thrift shops

These are more challenging, because you need to be more discerning. At thrift shops there's brilliance to be found. Stuff that no one has, that a vintage-clothes dealer might overlook, interesting things with a twist. There are wonderful, eccentric thrift shops and dull ones, and some go through phases. One thrift shop was so famous for its "everything £2" sales that no one went in the rest of the time and a £2 price policy became a fixture until the shop's closure. Being in Bayswater, a swanky area of London, fabulous McQueen dresses and Dior suits had been donated there, so you could pick them up for a couple of bucks. That sounds unusual, but if you're plugged into the thrift shops in your area, mad opportunities do come up.

Iris scores with perfect-fit pink corduroy flares.

The whole browsing thing should be peaceful and relaxed, you in your own bubble.

You can tell from doing a quick round of a shop, including glancing at the accessories, whether you want to dive in.

Give up on an uninspiring thrift shop quickly, or your eyes will cross and you will start to consider '90s sequined evening dresses and club-wear, or a Warehouse top from 2004 with beads and a stain. Never get anything with a stain.

How good a thrift shop is depends where it gets its stock from, what its pricing policy is and how much it just wants to shift stuff.

The more packed with stuff the shop is, the more likely you are to find a gem; the less packed, the easier it is to see if there aren't any.

If you're not quite sure and it's cheap, then buy it. It's for a good cause. Have a constantly rotating cast-off bag at home.

Doubt your friends' opinions about what you should get. In the meantime, insist that those Rasta pantaloons are soooo them.

Things that look bizarre and unflattering on the hanger might be well designed and genius on.

After a long session in a small shop, take mountains of stuff into the changing room, pissing off the staff. In most thrift shops, just about everything you do will piss off the staff, but they're friendly when you buy something.

A lot of synthetic lingerie and nightwear has ancient Egyptian-style pleats, worth looking out for in thrift shops. If you dye them deeper colors, they instantly look "day wear." A black pleated nightie looks *très* "Gothic Ancient Greek" (an important new genre).

Thrift-store tourism

One of the best things about thrift shops is exploring them when you're out of your neighbourhood. Any provincial town in Britain has a thrift shop, which doubles as an interestingly mundane museum of the area. We take trips together, motivated by thrifting, and other than the odd punch-up over bric-a-brac, we have the best time. We feel we've really seen Weston-super-Mare, Atlantic City, New Mexico, Las Vegas and Connecticut, and are boosted by our amazing finds in these places.

A thrifter never misses an opportunity. "Stop the car!" If you're in uncharted territory and spot a thrift shop, yard sale, try not to screech to a halt, and don't panic and then have an argument with your boyfriend about driving while circumnavigating the one-way system to find a parking space.

Berlin, Montreal, Cape Town… Houston has loads in the Montrose area; one in particular is called '50s, '60s, '70s; Knoxville, Tennessee. Provincial UK towns are cheaper than cities: the Cotswolds, seaside towns like Bexhill-on-Sea.

Cruising around New Mexico. Stop the car!

The holiday eye

On holiday, one has a relaxed, more assured eye. Wherever you go, what's normal will be different from what's back home. A cheap shop in Spain is somehow more fascinating.

SPECIALTY SHOPS

They're everywhere: sports, camping, workwear, pet, sailing, fishing, "adult," dancing, uniforms — army, navy, cook, nurse, postman — retro secondhand and ethnic specialty shops. You might not be their target demographic, which may make them seem uninviting, but take the plunge into the unknown waters of a goth store, or a ballet shop, or a very religious-looking Syrian shop, and your life is enriched. That's where you can score the really good finds. These shops often don't have websites, so you'll need to look for them in the Yellow Pages — who said it was defunct?!

Department stores for crisp white cotton nighties.

A well-fitting nurse's dress is simple and chic. Dye it.

New York garbagemen have great cut pants — straight leg, high waist.

Indian shops for everything cotton in pretty patterns, especially scarves. Also for classic sock slippers and silver jewelry.

'40s/'50s retro shops for beautiful one-offs. Ski and sports wear is worth checking out. Escape into a more innocent era, subversively.

'60s retro shops for neck scarves, jeans, top-quality old denim jackets and pimp coats.

Outdoor, rambling and climbing gear is made for people who not only like doing those things but get around to it. Mountaintop air and fashion somehow contradict each other, thank heavens, so designs are refreshingly "square."

Go Cossack, it's so romantic.

Men's army sweaters with patches at the elbows and buttons on the shoulders can be found at most uniform shops.

Sailing: the cap, the deck shoes, the Breton top, the Brigitte Bardot.

Waxed fishing sweater. They have a great texture to look at, if not to touch — rather like a straw bag. Wear with a cotton turtleneck underneath.

Character shoes, tango shoes in white satin that you can dye any color, ballet flats, body stockings, super-opaque tights in white, pale pink and black from dance shops.

Pastures are rich for speciality gloves, whether for riding, golfing, driving, being a bridesmaid, or wearing them anyhoo.

Workwear boots can look totally cool; maybe you can pull off white hygienic nurses' shoes with black trousers.

Vintage shops for men often have classic tweeds for women too. Old bespoke men's coats, tuxedos, shoes, and shirts are often small enough for women.

Chinese shops are great for their padded brocade silk jackets and vests – cozy with jeans.

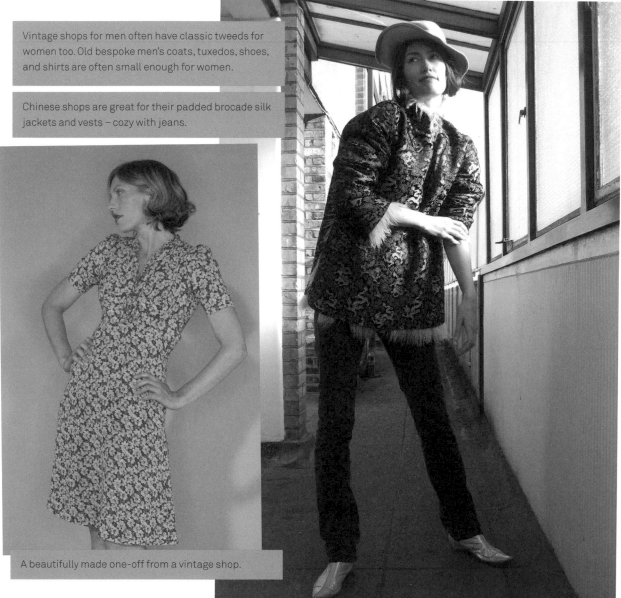

A beautifully made one-off from a vintage shop.

DITA VON TEESE

Burlesque performer.

Who inspires you?

I'm inspired by old movies. I love Marlene Dietrich, Greta Garbo and Rita Hayworth, especially in the film *Cover Girl.* Miniature top hats and veils. It is like a wonderful film of fashion. I love *An American in Paris* too. I wanted to dress like an elegant woman. My aunt Opal was out there. Extravagant. Eccentric. Always covered in costume jewelry. I was fascinated by her. My family may have thought she was vulgar, but to me she was beautiful. She had a profound effect and influence on the way I think about beauty and style. I'm inspired by art and by historic fashion. I studied history of fashion, which I loved. I'm also into modern designers like Moschino and Marc Jacobs, but my real love derives from the past. I can do modern but I've learned how to dress head to toe in vintage fashion. I love mixing old hats and clothes with modern pieces.

Do you see yourself as retrogressive?

Yes, but what I like about retro fashion is the emphasis on shape and the thin waist. If I wear pants they will be Dietrich pants.

Your look is all about old-fashioned femininity…

I love how what you wear governs the way you carry yourself, and the way you sit. A lot for me is to do with posture. One's entire demeanor changes depending on what one is wearing. I like clothes that make me look, sit and walk like a lady.

How important are fit and quality to stylishness?

Important. What I love is the quality of fabric. Things were made out of such opulent fabrics in the past. Silks, velvets, taffeta… those kinds of fabrics now are only found in couture. My style is about things fitting well. Fit is important in every way to my style. I wear corsets so the waist fits perfectly.

Where are your secret places to shop?

I love the thrill of the hunt. I like to look in small cities — that's where you find gems. Santa Monica has an amazing clothing expo; different sellers come from all over the country for one incredible giant swap fest.

What about accessories?

I love to accessorize. There's a fine line to be drawn, however. It is important to know when to say when.

When you're home, do you ever just wear sweats?

I have a cashmere robe I wear…

Rita inspires Dita.

EBAY — A MASSIVE GLOBAL CASBAH

Do you have a yen for pink stilettos? On eBay, the most specific thing you can think of could literally be at your fingertips. Say you fancy a Jimi Hendrix makeover. Instantly possible in cyberspace. For what we've been talking about in this chapter — having a direct relationship with what clothes you choose to have, rather than one filtered with pressure through mainstream commercial interests — the Internet is the ultimate solution. Make what's on your mind show up at your doorstep, from anywhere in the world. EBay and digital cameras are incredible for allowing secondhand clothes to be bought and sold this way.

Go to *ebay.com* and remember to press the "worldwide" button — that way you only get items that the seller is prepared to ship to you.

You can type in looks such as "pirate," check the list of categories at the side and choose which one fits.

It's good for large sizes. Sizes from different countries can be converted on *www.85b.org/dress_conv.php*

Check shipping costs before buying, and keep an eye on the customer feedback for the seller.

The most unboring way to browse is to trust your intuition — if you like something then go into the seller's "shop" or list. Otherwise you're stuck in "pink cardigan" or whatever your search is for.

Things tend to come ironed and washed.

If you're selling, don't put a reserve on: just have your minimum as the starting price.

Color coordination is easy. Whether it's a plain t-shirt in a specific shade of verdant green or a peachy pink cluster of roses, you can hunt it down.

If you live in the backwoods, you can buy a whole new wardrobe for a quarter of the price.

If you have your exact measurements, you can get tailored clothes on the net for a fraction of the price.

CHLOË SEVIGNY

How has your background influenced your style?

My father was very stylish; I guess it was a lifestyle. He was in the military so perhaps that added to his style. Seeing him, and the way he presented himself, made me think in the same way, whereas my mother was a bit more laid-back about clothes. My aunt was also quite chic. She wore a black turtleneck; always had nice hair and tortoiseshell glasses. She had that kind of casual American chic — very clean. Chic in her own way; she was inspirational to me. She had vintage Pucci dresses that she gave me; she would always give me tons of hand-me-downs. I remember this white houndstooth YSL shirt that she gave me when I was in high school. She was my introduction to high fashion and brand names.

I was obsessed by *Little House on the Prairie* when I was seven years old. I would only wear dresses and little booties. I would sleep in a little white nightcap like they wore on the show. I was obsessed! I used to love the Esprit catologues; the zany, strange combinations that were put together; a patterned shirt with an Argyle sweater.

Little House on the Prairie.

My brother was into skateboarding and that had a big influence on me; I would wear purple and pink checkered Vans. I was always inspired by images from pre-teen movies and music videos. My influences are from kind of everywhere.

What are you into at the moment?

Grunge. I'm also inspired by fashion magazines. I love big shapes too. Dior capes, bulbous coats, a huge knit hat. Sometimes I'm ahead of fashion, sometimes at the same time — but I just kind of wear it my way, and make it my own. Even if I buy new, I never wear it, it just stays in my closet. I just feel happier in secondhand clothes. I always have.

What do you think a stylish person's relationship to fashion is?

With high fashion I think it depends on your budget. I'm always more inclined to buy vintage high fashion rather than current high fashion — but I think you can be very inspired by the collections and by magazines, and make your own interpretations, which is what I did in high school. I remember when I started reading the British magazines like *ID* and *The Face*, and it opened up a whole new thing for me. I was photographed for these magazines, so I would be, like, "what's this?" Someone once said to me that I was avant-garde trendy! I've never felt trendy.

Marlene Dietrich

One of the most unique things about your style is how knowing it is — when you reference looks it is done in such a layered and understood way. Can you explain this?

I was always obsessed with youth culture and how different types of kids would present themselves to identify with other tribes. There was such a fine line between one or the other... you know, the new waves or the goths. The distinction was in a style of shoe, a certain length of skirt. That is just me, I just used to obsess over this.

Name one of your style icons.

Marlene Dietrich, who actually used to wear all her own clothes in her movies, and used to wear the same thing over and over. She found her look and just stuck to it. I read somewhere that when you find your hairdo you should always stick to it, because then you never age — anyone from Anna Wintour to Patti Smith does that. I think that was part of Marlene's thing as well — so that she always looked the same, and didn't age. But she would always have feathers around her collars to reflect the light. She was very sophisticated.

CHLOË SEVIGNY

What do you think of stylists dressing celebrities, which is so huge now?

I can understand that girls are too busy to do it themselves. But the way that they are celebrated for being amazing for throwing these looks together, when in fact a stylist took four hours to throw it together — that kind of irritates me. I feel like people are getting credit where it is not really due. Whereas with me, I go online to look at all the collections, to see what is available for red-carpet events.

Does skinniness make being stylish easier?

I don't necessarily think so. I have some friends who are quite small, Tara Subkoff, for example. She is one of the most stylish women I know. She looks better than a six-foot-tall model because she knows how to put herself together. She paints herself up like a pretty little picture. I love to look at her beacuse she always has something interesting going on; a braid in her hair, or the texture of a dress. That's what I love about looking at people who take pride in how they look, and who are into style: they are like eye candy. I love to look at beautiful things.

What do accessories mean to you?

Accessories are always hard for me. I'm a bit baffled by them. I always see myself as having a very big face, and strong features, so if I do accessories I tend to pile them on in quite a big way. I always actually want to wear something delicate, but it just doesn't feel right on me. I'm still trying to figure out jewelry.

What do you think of the white T-shirt?

I do like the white T-shirt, it's a classic — especially if it's a bit worn and thin. I have a problem in that I have boobs and sometimes that's hard with the white T-shirt. I do think it is harder to dress with breasts. Jackets and clothes generally look better with no boobs — the clothes just hang more beautifully. White T-shirts always look great on girls who don't have to wear bras.

Chloë with Harmony Korine.

How important are fit and quality to stylishness?

I think you can never go wrong with natural fibers. You know, like a nice cashmere sweater, or cotton pants or shirt. A big weird rayon shirt is just not going to look as good. I think that is a good tip for thrifting too; to always look out for nice natural fibers: 100 percent cashmeres, wools and silks.

Do you think you can acquire style? How do you think it works?

I've never seen someone that I thought had bad style all of a sudden have good style — so I think it is probably something you're born with, and maybe it is about being exposed to things that you weren't before… but I do think you're probably born with it. Don't you? I think a lot of people who are very stylish are creatively inclined, you know? They think about things in different ways than people who aren't.

Chloë!

Chloë on a style skyscraper.

What do you think of the red-carpet look?

Again, I think people do too much; too much hair, too much makeup — and that can ruin a dress. You can have a beautiful dress, and you do crazy hair and makeup and it can just look very plastic. I remember seeing Lauren Hutton at the last Oscars and she was wearing a YSL tuxedo with an ethnic bag. She didn't have much makeup on, and she looked beautiful and she got slammed left and right, and I thought she looked better than anyone else on the carpet. She just looked natural. I think people have to let their natural beauty shine through more.

ACCESSORIES

Accessories are just brilliant. They're pure fun. What shape your body is matters less and there are no rules. You are both putting across a feeling, and enhancing yourself.

A single accessory could be everything. In this case, a black ribbon tied in a bow or a bolo tie would also do the trick for a renegade, frontier-gambler look.

Have loads, piles, *tons* of accessible accessories. Don't cull — you can't have too many. Your collected moods make your wardrobe work. They're the easiest way to make anything look stylish and "you." Even if you're going through a phase of wearing just a gold chain, having the choice of accessories gives you the option of becoming anything.

Stylishness hinges on the edges and details, whether it's the crispness of your white cotton, or the garishness of your Denise Huxtable head-scarf. Choosing accessories is all about having clarity in the delicate balance between excitement and restraint. They can be the final carving out of yourself as fascinating, chic and self-contained. Refine it, with subtle tweaks and twists, down to little drop earrings and a hair bun if that's absolutely you, or a single bold accessory — a scarf, brooch or hat could be all the doctor ordered.

Having said that, don't be cowed by that fashion thing of "don't overdo it." Says who? If you feel like overdoing it, then overdo it. Cowardliness with accessories shows. With a clear, bold commitment to your vision, rampant accessories can be magical; heaping it on can be a trademark. Look at Lagerfeld's hands, or Ladakhi women who wear their wealth in the form of lapis, turquoise, coral, freshwater pearls and silver.

With functional accessories, let your clothes' style seep into your lifestyle and get on top of minor practicalities with panache.

Can't fail with...

There are accessories which, if they feel right, you can wear with anything: red lipstick, gold hoop earrings, cowboy boots, a delicate gold necklace, sneakers (low- and high-tops), a brown leather belt with brass buckle, fresh flowers in your hair.

Above: going for it. Right: refining it.

HEADGEAR — FRAMING YOUR FACE

Top, left-right: The Queen does baboushka; Anita Pallenberg; Mischa Barton; designer Nana Aganovich; woman with cowboy hat. Middle: Daisy de Villeneuve; Cossack hat; cozy ears; earrings and wisps of hair with headscarf. Bottom: Chloë Sevigny in beret with brooch; Grace Jones; a nice way to pin your headscarf; army cap on Tara Subkoff.

The Queen knows how to wear a scarf.

A fisherman's cap with jeans. A sailor cap or Greek shipping cap can look great if worn loosely. Think Dietrich, Debbie Harry, '80s supermodel in Lycra.

A classic straw hat or felt Fedora that you can tie your own fabric around: velvet or polka dot or leopard or whatever, to suit the occasion and your outfit. Maybe add a flower too. Simple thin rope looks very cool: three strands of it, to be precise!

A ribbon around your head, velvet or satin, of any color, to the side, or even behind the ear, worn with panache.

A camouflage cap is a great look… it harks back to all kinds of ideas (a slice of *Apocalypse Now*, tough, armed with a whole load of attitude and savviness) and looks very sexy. We recommend wearing it with something very simple: a plain black, simple jersey dress, something kind of downbeat.

The beret — practical, flexible. Try different shapes on your head.

The softness of fur around the face in the harshness of winter is instantly beautifying.

An unscratchy wooly hat and scarf is practical chic.

HANDBAGS

The really great thing about the explosion in popularity of luxury bags is that it has reinvigorated the whole fashion industry with quality and high-level workmanship.

No one used to give a hoot about bags, but now people go to Topshop and spend £50 on an outfit, then go and spend £900 on a celebrity-endorsed, large bag with Prada written on it. Having the latest, posh power bag gives an overriding identity to the owner, that of "player" and defiance. But it makes sense not to buy too much into the elitist, materialistic, celebrity-aspiring phenomenon that it's all about.

The LL Bean Boat and Tote bag (*llbean.com*) is the original classic and they'll monogram your initials on.

If you carry around a laptop, get an interesting bag for it off the Internet.

If you always remember to scan the bags in thrift shops, you'll always have an enviable one.

A see-through bag! So much easier to find stuff in.

Conspicuous labels can be funny, but to spend a lot of money on ironic clothes and accessories labels one a fashionista.

SHOES

They say an awful lot about somebody, everyone
agrees on that. If you can't afford YSL, it's a bit of a slog
to find good ones. Shoes are the easiest thing to make
ugly and unsexy, simply by not sticking to a classic
shape. They stop saying good things when the design
is too weird. Major shoe chains are surprisingly and
horribly "avant garde": They're always trying to think
up new modern designs when they should just forget
it and go the Italian route. It's interesting that they
haven't realized that, or perhaps there's a conspiracy.
These shops are simultaneously filled with shoes of
the latest inappropriate hybrid of classic designs or
ridiculously extreme styles — the toes are too elon-
gated and pointy, or too rounded or square. The lines
of the shoes contradict where the eye wants to go —
if it looks good from one angle, it's nearly always dis-
appointing from another. Though the odd gem shines
through, it's easier perhaps to stick to classics.

CAMILLA NICKERSON

Camilla Nickerson, fashion director of *W* magazine, is one of fashion's most powerful and intelligent people.

I grew up in a time when there was a lot of fashion, and then through the '90s it was very anti-fashion; it all became about the body in the clothes more than the clothes themselves. Right now I see people who were born in the '90s embracing fashion. It's a great time, you see it everywhere, it's really apparent. And in the same way that you can have someone on their cell phone, emailing and listening to an iPod all at the same time, well, that's how layered fashion and style is, how rich it is right now.

The younger generation is discovering fashion in a fresh way. They really embrace design and understand it. They mix it in a very, very rich way. I just think people are so formal today. Information is much easier to come by. On eBay you can buy everything, you can wish for something and it's instantaneous. People can read and "get" you instantly. People calling out are fully "audible." You'll know what book they're reading or what music they are listening to.

Stylish to me is the weird mix that represents the cultural shift. I get excited when I see it moving a boundary, or changing the shape of the body, or defining a new silhouette. And that passing into their lifestyle, in the same way.

I do think that, often, creative people are stylish. There are style mavens, but then there is a guy who works in a garage upstate and he's always what I consider immensely stylish. He has a gas attendant's uniform, and he looks like he's walked out of the '50s; he's consistent, and very chic.

Yesterday, I was talking to somebody, they'd just been to Africa, they were driving through the Serengeti and they hadn't seen anyone for a day, and suddenly they come across this Maasai family. One of the dudes has got a denim jacket on and he's standing, leaning on his stick as if he's in a [fashion photographer] David Sims photograph, and, you know — how did he get it?

I think if you promote your mind outward, constantly questioning, constantly looking and constantly informing your world, then you have style. You can show you are healthy and exciting, if you can get it together.

My style tip is: TRY A BIT HARDER!

BELTS

Anita Pallenberg models a worn brown leather belt with a brass buckle — a staple.

Another bit of dash, shaping you and adding to your mood. A good, hardy belt used for practicality is grounding. You can make anything fit you with a belt, and a belt can go over anything: coat, cardigan, shirt, dress or jeans, whether hanging on your hips or nestled, comfortably, at your waist. If you have large breasts, belts bring your shape back in when you're in danger of becoming tent-like. Elastic waist-cinching belts with large buckles act as comfy corsets and don't dig in as your tummy grows over the day.

JEWELRY

Jewelry is ornament, there to display something. It's nonessential for practicalities of life, but handy for peacocklike seduction.

Pearls lived around every self-respecting style icon's neck up until the '60s, and that über-trendy, the Queen of England, still wears 'em. With a lovely white summery cotton dress, a white shirt, or dress them up with a classic tux. They have such a great history — make them your own.

Apart from the risk of getting mugged, we like the idea of having beautiful jewels rather than a savings account.

If you are going out to a fancy do, and you are wearing a tux-style black jacket — get a white flower to put in the top pocket.

Iris's single gold sovereign earring, for luck.

Simple circular or oval blobs-of-plastic earrings, clip-on or not, any color.

Bamboo bangles with rolled-up white shirtsleeves. Intricate hoop earrings in Indian gold, which is a distinctive, rich yellow color (pop to Jaipur in India for these and gold chains). Two bracelets, one on each wrist, worn over the cuffs of a day sweater.

Always keep an eye out for brooches in thrift shops, they're such a nice detail. On a plain cashmere sweater they can look tremendously chic, and the look twists to become utterly individual.

A big ethnic necklace looks great with a very simple top but better with a busy one.

Tons of thin gold bangles.

A purple heart:
Find bravery like the lion in *The Wizard of Oz*.

Signet ring: aristocracy, gangster, gypsy.

Gold jewelry in Sierra Leone.

Niki Jolliffe

Eclectic coordination.

Bonnie's jewelry is made super-tasteful by being worn with a check shirt.

British *demimondaine* Gaby Deslys.

Maasai tribeswoman.

Bay's signet ring.

The Queen.

SCARVES

A scarf 'round the neck puts across surprisingly powerful messages. It can transform your look into combinations of air stewardess, '50s French chic, cowboy, folk costume, glamour puss, biker, and prepster. It can bring the colors and textures you're wearing together, and reach out to anyone who observes you. A scarf is important, but it's not as if your whole identity rides on it. Ideas should be fun and throwaway.

Wear the collars of your shirt up with a printed silk scarf worn, shawl-style, on the inside. A chic riding look. With the shirt buttons slightly open it looks relaxed too.

A loved, longish, narrow scarf, wound round the neck once so both ends fall down the front, is hippy or glam-rocker.

Is the scarf there? Definitely.

We call the polka-dot scarf a basic accessory.

The white T-shirt with a simple chiffon scarf tied round the front. Maria Callas did this, and it adds drama to the classic, pared-down, simple look.

The corners of a little crêpe scarf tied round the neck can point out at angles to the side or back.

Twist the corners of a neckerchief for maximum cowboy kudos (see Joan Jett on page 67).

Diana pulls off a proportion coup.

A huge, soft, lightweight but warm blanket scarf can be wrapped around the head and neck in at least eighty-three different ways and is handy for traveling.

OTHER ACCESSORIES

Handkerchief. Carrying around a square of beautifully patterned silk or monogrammed white cotton is one of those lifestyle-enhancing touches. Sticking out of your pocket, whipped out with a flourish in moments of need, using hankies is a chic habit. If an inheritance opportunity comes up, then pounce.

Fans: very Japanese, very rococo, very Lagerfeld.

One small feather.

The hairclip.

Bauer side-by-side rollerskates.

Shoelaces — nice and new and white, or any style from *theshoelaceplace.com.*

Socks. Sometimes just wearing your holey black ones with trousers is all you're going to do, isn't it? And that's fine. We don't want to press you into obsessing about every detail. But the smallest well-thought-out touches are noticed, on some level. Good slouchy socks are raunchy.

Transfer tattoos, vintage styles.

A leather Filofax gets better and better with age.

Friends, grandparents, babies, lovers.

How to carry a baby in Sierra Leone.

KELIS

Are you big on accessories?

I'm an overly-accessorizing kind of person by nature, I can't live without them. I think you can wear a cute white T-shirt and great jeans — and if you have the right bag, belt, glasses, scarf and jewelry you can look amazing. It really can be as simple as a Gap T-shirt and some Levi jeans. That's what it's about. Anyone can go out and buy a four-thousand-dollar outfit — but a person with real style needs to be able to make a white T-shirt and pair of jeans look stylish… you're a real person; that's important.

Who and what are your sources of style inspiration?

Oh, man, it's everything — old movies and old TV shows. I used to love Krystle Carrington from *Dynasty* — I started wearing pearls, and those huge puff silk blouses because of her. Tina Turner has fantastic style… Seeing how stuff was worn in the '40s, '50s and '60s and making those things part of my everyday life. Sometimes I see someone on the street, and everything they have on could be totally wrong, and one thing might catch my eye and it's like, "Oh my God" that done a bit differently would look brilliant. I find every day inspiring; even when it rains I don't have to look bad, if I have really cute rainboots and a great raincoat.

Do you think you have to be skinny to be stylish?

No, I think you have to be fit, and in a good mental state to feel good about yourself. I'm never going to be skinny — I'm toned and I'm in shape. I have a butt, I have arms. I am a full-figured woman. It's about being realistic — as long as you know your body you can make things look good on you. If I wear an empire dress it looks like I'm wearing a tent. I would love to wear them, but they just don't look good on me. Sometimes I'll see something, and think "God, that's fantastic!" and then I put it on I'm like, "No way." It may look great on someone else, but it doesn't look good on me. I never look at another woman and think, "Oh, I want to wear it just like that" — that would be depressing. I don't look like anyone else, I look like me.

How much does your heritage and the environment in which you grew up affect your style?

I grew up in Harlem, Manhattan. I think black people in general have a strong sense of style and fashion is important to us as a culture. I was inspired by the people around me when I was growing up. I am a black singer, twenty-six years old, and lots of younger girls are now looking at me to see what I'm wearing. I think it is a cycle. I didn't grow up rich so I learned how to shop, and how to get the look that I wanted without spending tons of money — so I still do that in my life now. I think a good shopper can shop anywhere — from thrift stores to Topshop, up to designer.

Linda Evans as Krystle Carrington in *Dynasty*.

Tina Turner

How do you dress when you are performing?

I wear things that are going to catch the light — I've got to wear stuff that's going to stay looking good the whole way through.

You are married to Nas, who has great style too. Are you influenced by the way he dresses?

I am very singular in the way that I dress, and I don't ask for or take much advice on the way that I look. Even if someone says I look great in something, if I don't feel it, I don't wear it. Nas has a great sense of style, but he just doesn't care in the same way that I care about clothes. If I shop for him, he thinks that's great because then he doesn't have to. He's pretty relaxed about it. It's a rare occasion that he goes out shopping.

K E L I S

Birds by Annabel Astor.

Brooke Shields

Were you an outsider when you were growing up?

I was totally an outsider — totally out there. But I thought I was really stylish! I shaved my head when I was twelve. And after that I never looked like anybody else. I would just do my own thing.

What are your style tips?

Only buy things that you absolutely love, even if it's just a T-shirt; you will always end up wearing that T-shirt. Abercrombie and Fitch does the best basics — brilliant fitting T-shirts and sweatpants. Dress appropriately for the occasion — if you wear a clubbing kind of dress going to a bar mitzvah, it's totally not going to look appropriate. Dressing is such a great way for women to express who they are, and how they feel on that day. Don't walk out of the house until you feel great.

MAGIC

You do believe in magic! It is there, in the imagination, to create.

Archetypes

There's so much symbolism in the clothes you wear: representations of archetypes that people pick up at an unconscious level — the level a magician or hypnotist works on.

> **"Walk on a rainbow trail; walk on a trail of song, and all about you will be beauty. There is a way out of every dark mist, over a rainbow."**
>
> Navajo song.

> **"The moment one gives close attention to anything, even a blade of grass, it becomes a mysterious, awesome, indescribably magnificent world in itself."**
>
> Henry Miller

Iris as The Vamp:
Tight black dress or suit, a splash of red (lips, nails or shoes) and a cold, ravenous glint in the eye.

The Activist.

Tara as The Belly-Dancer.

The '80s All-American Girl.

Francesca as The Office Seductress.

The Madonna.

Nana as The Artist's Muse.

Oonagh The Sage.

The Dreamer.

Some typical examples of typical examples

The Prickly New York Art Dealer: In drapey charcoal Japanese designs.

The Prepster: Seersucker suit, sneakers, sarcasm.

The Street 'Tute: This archetype's ultimate expression comes together in Bratz dolls.

15th Century Chinese Fairy: Feminine colors, billowing fabrics, sashes and ribbons.

The Duckie Dale: Piano keyboard tie, two-tone suit, trilby, and crepe-soled '50s shoes.

The Girl Scout: If that's what you were or wanted to be.

The Finger-Clickin' Beatnik: Tight-fitting black from neck to toe. Intellectual hair.

The Wino: Old tailored suit and sneakers with no socks.

The Sweet Old Lady: We say the raglan-sleeve old-lady coat is an absolute, complete, and utter must — or else.

The Old-Fashioned Governess: Calf-length tweed skirt, roll-neck sweater and matching accessories. This is the same look for "the superhero in mufti."

The Office Worker: Efficient secretary, power bitch, brainiac, wheeler-dealer, mousy secret-sex-fiend etc.

The Sage Robes: No shoulder structure, natural colors.

The '50s Pinup: Neck scarf, tight sweater, hot pants, stiletto heels.

The Golfer: So much to draw on from over the ages. Check pants, tassel shoes, Argyle tank top, gloves with holes in them.

The Circus Girl: Sequins, feathers, tights and pumps.

The Spacewoman: Silver.

The Cowgirl Teddy Girl: Jeans with belt at waist, a sweet blouse or shirt, high ponytail, '40s heels (if jeans rolled up to calf), neckerchief.

The Cave Woman: Skins and leather.

The Feisty Teenage Girl who Pulls Chewing Gum out in a String: A tank dress, a belt slung low and new sneakers.

The Glam-Rocker: Beautiful '30s sequin jacket with casual clothes, scrunched-up sleeves.

The Auntie: Start thinking from flowery cardigan.

The Wild Sex Beast: Studiedly tousled. Kim Basinger.

The '80s All-American Girl: Think Farrah Fawcett in cut-offs and flicky hair.

The schoolgirl or the nun: Puritan starched cotton. A very powerful archetype!

Iris as The Sailor.

Laura as The Governess.

Tara Subkoff as The Spring Bunny.

Joan Collins as The '50s Pinup.

Catherine Deneuve as The Opera-Goer.

Laura as The Captain.

The Mysterious Eastern Woman.

THE MAGICAL, TRANSFORMATIVE POWER OF STYLE

Archetypes aren't just for pervs who fantasize about severe and strict nurses, they help you focus on what you're putting across. This is where an imaginative eye for what's classic comes in handy. If you want to wear open-toed, high-heeled mules, then bouffant hair too could be consistent with a '60s, Nancy Sinatra–esque look. Being stylish is a way to project whatever we like, to be who we want to be in our fantasies and to manipulate reality. It's amazing how what you wear puts you into a role. With the perfect, simplest pair of pointy black stilettos you're immediately "focused" and "sharp." You can wear a "suit disguise" to come across as more businesslike than you think you are. The authoritativeness of a uniform is the ultimate example, or the ceremonial, symbolic and opulent dress that dignifies royalty, and priests of all religions. Clothes can stop you being arrested. You feel much more in character if you buy an authentic dress from the '40s rather than "getting the look" from Karen Millen or Oasis.

This person must be important.

Melanie Griffith's *Working Girl* found success with a "suit disguise."

ANGELA BUTOLPH

UK Fashion guru from TV and radio.

I think being true to yourself is overrated. It's much more fun to be your alter ego; it's good to be your imaginary best friend. One of the things that appeals to me is the Mr Benn [British children's book and television character] scenario, coming out of your everyday life by putting on a costume, projecting into a new world. People forget how powerful putting clothes on as costume can be.

Your clothes can dictate your mood and your day, just as listening to particular music can. Wear something slinky if you're feeling fat; ask what mood you'd like to be in. No one is just one thing. Dressing up helps you discover yourself. You'll never know if you're a floozie if you don't try out that side of you.

Treating clothes as the grown-up version of the child's dressing-up box.

Recently I've appeared as "early '90s Rebecca," "discontented teenager Rebecca," "gypsy Rebecca" — a long-standing favorite — as well as "put-together market editor Rebecca" — a character I have to play more and more often these days due to my work!

Rebecca Guinness, fashion editor

Glamour

Glamour is such a good word. In olden days, glamour was a magic charm that made the eye see something as fairer than it was. Women who seem to exist in a haze of glamour, like the Hollywood stars of the '30s and '40s, Cleopatra or Kate Moss, seduce their observers, casting a spell that magnifies and glorifies themselves. It's not necessarily arrogant to do this — it's uplifting for everyone.

Gloria Swanson

Kate and Johnny

MISS PIGGY

What is it like to be such a style icon?

Moi is a style icon? Oh, how wonderful! I knew I was a living legend and a towering diva, but I hadn't heard about "style icon!" Oh goodie. I'll have to get Kermie to take me somewhere extravagant to celebrate.

Style tips?

Never stand too close to *moi*; you'll suffer by comparison. Trust me on this. When you love yourself, you have a style that emanates from within, which is wonderful… unless, of course, you just ate onions. Moisturize constantly. I don't know why, but everyone looks better wet. Put hard work in, constantly maintain your image, update your look and destroy old photos that show you in spandex with big hair. Always be yourself. That way you won't have to go get everything monogrammed again and again. To *moi*, clothes are like friends — they should always compliment your appearance.

What are classic "Miss Piggy" items of clothing?

Moi adores silk-and-satin arm-length gloves. They're sort of a trademark for *moi,* so be prepared to pay royalties if you want to try this yourself. Pearls. And if I hear even *one* joke involving the phrase "… before swine," someone is going to be in for a world of hurt. I adore diamonds, but any high-priced gemstones will work if you cover yourself in enough of 'em.

If Kermit said he'd find it really sexy if you wore a sack dress and Birkenstock shoes with greasy hair and a middle part, would you?

For Kermie, *moi* would do anything. But if he actually said that, I might knock him around a bit just to make sure it wasn't mind control or food poisoning or something like that. Kermie always wears what I tell him to; that's why he hardly ever wears anything at all.

What's your relationship with fashion?

The fashion world looks to *moi* for inspiration, and I look to the fashion world for freebies. Fashion and *moi* have been close for years. In fact, I've been wearing clothes since just after I was born… which is unusual where I come from.

Examples of stylish women today.

Among today's entertainment and fashion stars, there are so many fabulous icons of style. There's *moi*, of course, and… well, there's … oh, what's her name… you know who I mean … gee, there must be someone else, right?

We've heard that you don't choose your clothes at all, that you use a stylist. In fact, we've heard that someone else pulls the strings and even puts words into your mouth. What do you say to that?

How dare *vous* even insinuate such a scurrilous rumour! Why, if my writers weren't on holiday this week, I'd send you a strongly worded letter. In lieu of that… HIIIIIIIIII-YAAAAAA!!

How to be glamorous

You need to be ambitious, both to counter the banal and to stretch your style, opening the gates to your grown-up version of fairyland, or plucking ideas from the firmament.

Secret personal references; with the practical thing of knowing what looks good on you.

Red-carpet "glamour" these days is not magical because it's not personal – the outfits are interchangeable. In fact, it is quite mundane.

A little touch could be entrancing, and incredibly empowering for you – for instance, being inspired by a film to wear a beret.

Always be thinking with a fresh eye, never in a style rut. Real enthusiasm is childlike and magical.

A trademark. Whatever you're wearing, a Veronica Lake hairdo turns heads.

Well, there are always those who cannot distinguish between glitter and glamour… the glamour of Isadora Duncan came from her great, torn, bewildered, foolhardy soul.

Dorothy Parker

Friends can enhance each other's glamour.

A twinkle is good, but it could just as easily be in the eyes.

Like classics, glamorous is whatever you decide it is. There's no contradiction between being incredibly glamorous and being a social worker who has no interest in jetting off to New York.

Glamour is about female wiles – a powerful, primeval, esoteric, "witchy," seductive thing. The wearing of feathers, teeth, fur, stones or wood represents powerful natural forces, even in our secular society.

Filmmaker Julia Jason

Glamour and the British

In Britain, stylishness is thought to be so linked with class that we're a nation of slobs out of rebelliousness. It's what gives us our style genius, too, but it needn't be that loaded. It is just good to look good.

Glam rock had roots in weird Olde English magick as well as '30s glamour, and *The Lord of the Rings*. It was all very accessible: Rhinestones and gold lamé were worn with jeans and if not platforms then sneakers and a wizard or bard hat; a feather boa was crudely worn with a T-shirt; glitter varnish with a suit vest. It was a pinch of fairy dust over grey, plodding life.

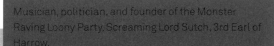
Musician, politician, and founder of the Monster Raving Loony Party, Screaming Lord Sutch, 3rd Earl of Harrow.

Fashion designer Bella Freud.

ZAC POSEN

How does one get inspired?

Stop reading fashion magazines, and think for yourself. Start going to museums and watching great films. Look at old clothes in vintage and secondhand stores. You've got to take risks. American women should put themselves on the pedestal that they put movie stars on. More people should be making their own clothing, and doing stuff with the clothes they have.

Why do you think not enough people are dong this?

People are probably not comfortable enough with themselves. A lot of people don't want to draw attention to themselves, so they're hiding. That relates to my philosophy — I love women, I don't make clothing for them to hide in. I'm making feminine, feminist clothing, without being pretentious.

You say you love women. Do you think there are people in fashion who don't?

A lot of people in fashion don't love women. They impose their own ego upon women, whether they're men or self-hating women.

ANNA PIAGGI

A fabulous Italian fashion intellectual who puts her theories into practice.

What inspires you?

I take inspiration from myself.

Do you ever just wear sweatpants and a sweater? Or do you always think about what you are going to wear?

I always think about what I'm going to wear — but it can be very practical. Quality of fabrics is very important: the weight and feeling on the body and the technicalities of the dress. I always keep an eye on the care and washing instructions. A dress, an item of clothing, is practically a part of your body, is another skin, and this skin has to make you feel at ease. It also has to make you happy and give you a glow. It is a mixture of being physical and even very personal. I have a very personal rapport with clothes — they are there to make me feel very much at ease. Not only do I go out, but I work. I believe very much in duplicity, double-dealing. The duplicity of having the great pleasure of wearing and the great pleasure of aesthetic. I am a living twin-set! My mother used to like me to be disciplined and conventional — I had a uniform, and I transformed the uniform in a kind of surrealistic way, in a kind of double reality. Double vision. But it is still a twin-set. My roots are in a twin-set.

What would be your style advice?

I think one should be completely relaxed, and a little bit off, asymmetric. Like building a geometric frame then destroying it.

Magical matches

White plastic.

Prince – Wow!

Peachy photographer Frances Armstrong-Jones.

A target and a team.

Karen

Amazing combinations

If magic is the inexplicably wonderful, then it exists in the way your scarf falls and clashes with your blouse. Concocting harmony or dissonance is effortless when inspired. Everyone has an individual way with colors. Here are some of our favorite magical mixups.

Dark grey and apricot.

Turquoise and lime green.

Pink and gold.

Red and pink is back.

The chic of a plastic children's pirate belt.

Black grosgrain ribbon tied in a bow at the top or side of your head.

A dark but verdant green with rich burgundy and bright brown – an obvious but much underused combination, good for velvet and corduroy.

Shoes with opaque tights *the same color* elongate the legs. It always looks a bit strange – in a good way, and you can pull off a bright color like red with dull clothes.

Navy, black and white, with gold buttons and jewelry, or pearls, or both.

Orsola de Castro, designer of From Somewhere, and editor of *VERY* magazine Uscha Pohl.

Purple ribbed turtleneck (because you just watched *Casino*) with a suede A-line skirt (because your mother is Danish). Native American chamois leather scarf. You pull it off.

IF YOU'VE GOT A STRONG GRIP ON THE REINS OF YOUR STYLE CHARIOT, IT CAN TAKE OFF, LIKE AT THE END OF *GREASE*

Pink tights. Black velvet dress with white lace.

Trilby with a multicolored sweater — very Peru.

Navy-and-cream stripes with red button earrings.

A corduroy dress in cheetah print.

A cream silk shirt with faded blue denim.

ANITA PALLENBERG

Who have you been inspired by over the years?

When I was a little girl I was inspired by Cleopatra, and those drapey-drapey Greek goddess portraits that I saw in museums — I admired all of that. The film stars I liked were kind of mannish, but with great style, like Joan Crawford, say; the furs! the lipstick! I thought Barbara Stanwyck was really great. From the '60s I liked Anouk Aimée in *La Dolce Vita*; she wore black shades, was kind of gender bender, and always dressed in black. Jeanne Moreau, of course, and Delphine Seyrig too. There was a period then, with all these stylish women, not so obvious as Audrey Hepburn, who always wore Balenciaga and Givenchy, and it was not so much the name connected to the face, as more the image, and that I admired. I didn't have much time for what was happening at Dior but Chanel always interested me — I always thought Coco Chanel very stylish. Of all the designers she was the only one who really understood comfort in a woman's body — for example, she did pockets. I can't live without pockets. She always did pockets.

Anita Pallenberg is generally thought of by those in the know as one of the great living style influences.

Do you think a lot about what you are going to wear?

I think a lot about what I am going to wear; I think at night before I go to bed, and then I think again in the morning. I kind of check myself; how I feel; where I'm at; what I want to represent; what I'm into; what I feel like wearing.

Jeanne Moreau

And today? Who do you find inspiring?

I think people have really become much more stylish. You can see a woman — a housewife, say — walking into a shop, and she will be wearing great sandals and will be put together in quite a nice way. There's so much more information available now than there was — in magazines, all around, where you learn how to do makeup, do the hair, wear the clothes. It is not exclusive anymore.

I think Charlotte Rampling has great style and the way Vivienne Westwood sticks to her guns is actually stylish — she looks like Elizabeth I; fantastic; orange hair, white makeup, an outrageous mix of clothes and curtains, different-colored socks, things like that; the end result is a kind of style. All the main designers now just copy her. And I like punk; punk was quite stylish too.

In the '60s you wore tons of ethnic stuff, and really mixed it up.

Yeah, but I don't think that was particularly stylish, that was more about dressing up. Some of those Afghani clothes were incredibly intricately made; the time it took to do the embroidery and lining — I can't say this is "stylish" — style is more bare, more down to the bone than that. A fur coat and lizard shoes — now that is stylish!

Joan Crawford

Liz Taylor as Cleopatra. Check out the armband.

What do you think of the idea that there is something dark about stylishness?

Anything that is to do with enhancing your appearance, not being natural and putting so much effort and obsession into the way you look is already quite dysfunctional. I think most women are happy to put on a T-shirt and jeans and get on with life — this obsession with keeping clothes and cherishing them is dark, I think.

ANITA
PALLENBERG

What are your favorite items of clothing at the moment?

I have rediscovered leopard. I am back on the hunt. But I think still my favorite dress that I've got that I never wear is a Pucci silk jersey dress. I have to know it is there.

What do you think of trendiness?

I quite like trendiness, actually. I like it when people are choosing what they are going to wear so carefully that they are almot manic. I like the attention to detail… buttons high up, and the type of suit on the guy.

Do you think people are born with style, or is something that can be acquired?

I think that there are people who are just born more gifted with style than other people. Today there is a kind of bombardment of everything. And sometimes people look really stylish almost by mistake. Style has nothing to do with consumerism and money. I have had lots of money at points in my life, but I never went to Dior or anywhere like that. I'd rather hunt it down in secondhand shops. The pleasure of finding something I've found that I like is infinitely more pleasurable than having a whole wardrobe presented to you by a stylist.

What do you think about accessories?

I love accessories. Now, I'm not so into clothes, but I'm into accessories — the bags, the shoes, the jewelry. At the moment I'm into little pumps and bags — no jewelry at all, because too many people wear it. I always try and do what other people aren't doing. If I see somebody walking with a pair of pants that I really liked the day before, and I don't like the look of that person, I'm just gonna stop wearing them completely. That's a bit of a drag.

Are fabric and detail important to you?

I love fabrics; silks. Lamé is my favorite. That is what I don't like about the second wave of hippiedom — the fabrics are just not good enough.

Practical style tips?

Keep your toenails clean! Belt it! Belt it wherever; the hip, waist. It's such a solution to an outfit to just belt it — always looks good. Add some jewelry, change your handbag — just tweak it.

One of Anita's influences is gangsters, in this case Chicago boss Sam Giancana. Check out the bracelet.

Did you have a dress-up box as a child?

I had my mum's. She had tons of lamé. And then later in life I went to an auction in Hollywood and bought Joan Crawford's old fur coats which all got destroyed in a fire.

What do you think about rock 'n' roll style?

I love it. I love it. The tight pants and all of that. I'm a sucker for it totally — I can't really resist someone who looks like that — scarves and hats and white shoes. I love the gangster look, too — and uniforms.

Do you always refer to the source of inspiration in your mind in relation to what you are wearing?

It isn't always just people, like Marilyn Monroe when she had a little white angora sweater and little black skirt. I also get off on fabrics and colors.

Do you get things customized?

I used to get shoes and boots customized. I would get nappa boots, and get buttons put on them up to the knee, up the side.

What is your favorite style decade?

The '40s. I like all the crêpe de Chine, and silk crêpes, with the pleat in the front. Some were floral, some were completely black, and then I love the libertine period — big shirts and pirate stuff, kind of seventeenth and eighteenth century. Big boots and hats... love all that too.

Do you ever feel like just getting rid of all your clothes — just wearing the same thing, and not even thinking about it?

At the moment I am into minimalism. When I went to India for six months, I was happy to get myself a new dress; clean, simple and fresh every day — the same with the kimono. I would like to get rid of all my wardrobe and just keep four pieces — and see them all in one neat line. It might just be a dream. But I like having a moody wardrobe — trying on five different jackets until one of them suits my mood.

Do you spend a lot of money on clothes?

I always try and spend less than a hundred pounds on clothes. I don't believe in really expensive clothes. Clothes for me have always had a personal value, never monetary. If I swing into that mode, that means that I've had it! If I like an expensive jacket on a friend of mine — I will make sure I find something like it that I love in a thrift shop.

Do you have an anecdote about clothes?

When me and Marianne [Faithfull] were talking about the old days once, she kept telling me that I was at the Joshua Tree with [country rocker] Gram Parsons. I kept saying to her that I couldn't remember — that I just knew that we hadn't been there together. She kept insisting that we had been there together. Eventually I got really frustrated, because I knew that I wasn't there, so I asked her what I was wearing, and she said that I had been wearing a red dress. I said "NEVER! I would never go in the desert wearing a red dress." The way I grew, historically and religiously — I would never have worn a red dress in the desert. That is how important clothes are to me. I can remember pretty much every piece of clothing that I ever possessed.

Is there something political about your style?

I've always been myself with my style. I've always done it. Someone found some clothes of mine that were in a box for thirty years. I looked at them, and it is basically the same thing that I am wearing today. The pants with long jackets, beautiful fabrics — very kind of simple style, so I think I do have that kind of political attitude towards clothes. I don't give a toss about what everybody else wears. I am also quite prudish. I don't like to uncover myself much. I think Cavalli type of clothes are really hideous. I'm a bit more religious with my clothes. Nuns I love the look of. The last time I went to Portobello market, out of all the girls I saw with their jeans, boots and little tops — the one that really struck me was a little Muslim girl. She had the whole gear, and just her ankles showed — just [a few inches] of skin and she was the most stylish of all. I think my prudish side comes from having grown up next to a convent; I always watched nuns running around and playing ball — it doesn't inhibit them to run around, doing whatever they have to do — with this look that I love. Yes, for me a lot of my identity is about what I wear. It is a statement about who I am.

There are no rules. The world is your oyster, whether you end up looking fabulously odd and asymmetrical or chicly reined in and conventional. When you listen to your own opinion, the possibilities are endless. Absorbing an old Cecil Beaton photo, you could be inspired to wear kid gloves in grey with pearl wrist buttons of an evening out, and why not? Limitlessness is an addictive fix.

Credits

Contents: Nico reclines, c.1996 © Nat Finkelstein/Retna. **Introduction**: Garfield T-shirt © Tom Craig/CD. **7**: Sudanese woman © Tom Craig. **8**: Ronnie Spector, 1982 © Lynn Goldsmith/Corbis; Elvis and actress Venetia Stevenson, 1957 © Bettmann/Corbis; Chloë Sevigny © 2006 Chloë Sevigny Archive. **9**: Niki Jolliffe © Jolliffe Archive; Polly Devlin © Garnett Archive; Theodora Brown © Jolliffe Archive. **10**: Aurora Papafava © Lucie Layers/CD; Karen Elson © BG/CD. **11**: The New York Dolls © Bob Gruen. **12**: Jeanne Moreau © Sunset Boulevard/Corbis; Janis Joplin © Baron Wolman; Iris Palmer © KJ/CD. **13**: Luella Bartley © David Sims/Luella Bartley; Zoot suit teenager, 1943 © Bettmann/Corbis; Jamie Lee Curtis in costume for *Blue Steel*, 1988 © Lynn Goldsmith/Corbis. **16**: Kate Moss at Women of Achievement Party at Buckingham Palace, 2004 © Pool/Corbis. **17**: Sophie Polotovich © Poppy de Villeneuve/CD. **19**: Liz Renay © Liz Renay Archive; Diana Vreeland © Andy Warhol/Corbis. **20**: Cecilia Dean © Annabel Mehran/CD. **21**: Karen Elson © Annabel Mehran/CD. **22**: Tracey Emin © Scott Douglas. **23**: Silhouette illustration © 2006 Lucie Layers **24**: River Phoenix in *Silent Tongue*, 1993 © Bureau L.A. Collection/Corbis.; Ségolène Royal, 2000 © Vernier, Jean-Barnard/Corbis Sygma. **25**: Sophie Dahl © BG/CD. **26**: Sofia Coppola, 2000 © Mark Stephenson/Corbis Sygma; Portrait of opera singer Lina Cavalieri, c.1901, by Giovanni Boldini; Ieva Imsa © KJ/CD. **27**: Emma Malin © Tom Craig/CD; Daisy de Villeneuve © Jan de Villeneuve. **28**: Mischa Barton © BG/CD; Marianne Faithfull, 1992 © Lynn Goldsmith/Corbis. **29**: English punk rockers, 1980 © Phil Schermeister/Corbis; Women in fancy dresses by Cecil Beaton, 1948 © Condé Nast Archive/Corbis. **30**: Annie Morris © Robin Katz; Paris & Nicky Hilton, Tiffany Limos and Mariah © Annabel Mehran/CD. **31**: Debbie Harry, 1978 © Lynn Goldsmith/Corbis. **32**: Woman in grey top © www.allheart.com; Lauren Hutton, © www.celebritypicturesarchive.com. **33**: Jeanne Moreau in a scene from *Jules et Jim* c.1961 © John Springer Collection/Corbis. **34**: Ieva Imsa © KJ/CD; Tape measure © Lucie Layers/CD. **35**: Drew Barrymore on the set of *Wishful Thinking*, 1995 © Mitchell Gerber/Corbis; Patti Smith © Lynn Goldsmith. **36**: Jacqueline Kennedy Onassis © Bettman/Corbis; Sherilyn Fenn in *Twin Peaks*, 1990 © Corbis/Sygma. **37**: Tights illustration © 2006 Lucie Layers; Mary Quant among models wearing her footwear, 1967 © Hulton-Deutsch Collection/Corbis. **38**: Ballet flats © KJ/CD; Gray Jolliffe © Jolliffe Archive; Lucie Layers © KJ/CD; Marcel Duchamp, 1927 © Bettmann/Corbis; Lindsay Wagner, 1978 © Lynn Goldsmith/Corbis. **39**: Carisa Glucksman © Tom Craig/CD; Mischa Barton © BG/CD; Jane Fonda in *They Shoot Horses, Don't They?*, 1969 © John Springer Collection/Corbis. **40**: Iris Palmer © KJ/CD. **41**: Mademoiselle Chanel, 1935, photographed by Man Ray © House of Chanel; David Bowie, *The Man Who Fell to Earth* poster. **42**: Rachel Weisz © Daisy Garnett; *Butterfly 8* illustration © 2006 Lucie Layers. **43**: Karen Elson © Karl Lagerfeld. **44**: Ramona's Rolex watch © KJ/CD; Ramona's Nikes © KJ/CD; Nana Oforiatta-Ayim © BG/CD; Hoodie girls © Vanessa Galvin, www.vanessagalvin.com; Charlotte Rampling and her son, Barnaby, 1974 © Alain DeJean/Sygma/Corbis; Queen Elizabeth II wearing Philip Somerville, 1989 © Tim Graham/Corbis. **45**: Laura Lauberte & Ieva Imsa © KJ/CD; Laura Lauberte © KJ/CD, Ramona Rainey in white jeans

© KJ/CD; Daryl Hannah, 1980 © Henry Diltz/Corbis; Niki Jolliffe © Jolliffe Archive. **46**: Princess Anne walking with daughter Zara Phillips © Tim Graham/Corbis; Jane Russell © Harris Tweed. **47**: Lucy Granville © Tom Craig/CD; Lady Maria-Carmela Hambleden © KJ/CD. **48**: Isabella Rossellini, 1980 © Lynn Goldsmith/Corbis; Laura Lauberte © KJ/CD. **49**: Kate Moss, 2003 © Condé Nast Archive/Juergen Teller. **50**: Laura Lauberte © KJ/CD; Bruce Lee illustration © 2006 Lucie Layers. **51**: Isabella Blow © Polly Braden, as part of *Matthieu Laurette presents WHAT DO THEY WEAR AT FRIEZE ART FAIR? 21–23 October 2005* (Daily guided tours of Frieze Art Fair led by international fashion experts Peter Saville, Isabella Blow and KJ & BG. Commissioned and produced by Frieze Projects); Duke and Duchess of Windsor with dogs, 1941 © Bettmann/Corbis. **52**: Mini kilt © KJ/CD; Ramona Rainey © KJ/CD. **53**: Beth Ditto, 2006 © KJ/CD; Mischa Barton, 2006 © Condé Nast Archive/Regan Cameron. **54**: Cheap Date crest © 2006 Lucie Layers. **55**: Debbie Harry © Bob Gruen; Bebe Buell, 1979 © Lynn Goldsmith/Corbis; Charlotte Cooper © Tom Craig/CD; Marilyn Monroe wearing USS Henley T-shirt, 1952 © Bettmann/Corbis; Karen Elson © Karl Lagerfeld; Mihda Koray © Tom Craig/CD; Iris Palmer's vests © KJ/CD. **56–57**: Interview with Karl Lagerfeld by BG, 2005 © British *Vogue*. **56**: Karl Lagerfeld © House of Chanel; Elvis Presley performing in comeback special, 1968 © Bettmann/Corbis. **57**: Karen Elson & Karl Lagerfeld © BG/CD. **58**: Mademoiselle Chanel, 1934, photographed by Cecil Beaton © House of Chanel. **59-69**: Letter illustrations © 2006 Danny Sangra. **60**: Strawberry Switchblade © Peter McArthur; Nancy Sinatra, 1968 © Bettmann/Corbis; Yadira Grant, 2006 © Tom Craig/CD; US convict © Poppy de Villeneuve; Convict escaping on a zebra illustration © 2006 Lucie Layers. **61**: Sewing box © KJ/CD. **62**: George Melly © BG/CD; Surrealist poets with women and dog, 1930 © Stefano Bianchetti/Corbis. **63**: All photos of Nana Oforiatta-Ayim and family © Oforiatta-Ayim Archive. **64**: Paris Hilton (long pinky orange chiffon dress) 2004 © Frank Trapper/Corbis; Paris Hilton x 2 (silver dress and pink profile pose) 2004 © Jim Ruymen/Reuters/Corbis; Paris Hilton (in shiny gold) 2005 © Rufus F. Folkks/Corbis, Paris Hilton x 2 (in magenta strapless minidress and with pink fake fur) 2004 © Nancy Kaszerman/Zuna/Corbis; Hearts © 2006 Lucie Layers. **65**: Bella Freud © Tom Craig/CD; Dr Alimantado album cover © Greensleeves Records; Bob Marley, 1980 © Lynn Goldsmith/Corbis; Jamaican family go to church © Daniel Laine/Corbis. **66**: Keith Richards, 1975 by Christopher Simon Sykes © Getty Images; Johnny Thunders © Bob Gruen. **67**: Elvis Presley, 1956 © Bettmann/Corbis; Joan Jett album cover © Blackheart Records. **68**: Amelia Earhart beside her plane, 1930 © Bettmann/Corbis; Lee Miller, 1929 © Condé Nast Archive/Corbis. **69**: Wardrobe © KJ/CD. **70-71**: Interview with Vivienne Westwood by BG, 2005 © *Vogue* Nippon. **70**: Vivienne Westwood © Corinne Day. **72**: The Sex Pistols © Bob Gruen. **73**: Bay and Kira at the Cheap Date Swap Shop (letters by Daisy de Villeneuve, poster by Marlon Richards) © Jim Jolliffe/CD. **74-5**: Selection of clothes © CD. **76**: Woman at Cheap Date jumble sale with "find" © Sam Pelly, www.sampelly.com; Chloë Sevigny © Chloë Sevigny Archive. **77**: Beth Ditto, 2006 © KJ/CD; Poly Styrene of X-Ray Spex, 1978 © Denis

Market © BG/CD. **79**: Max's Kansas City "Christmas Dinner," 1975 © Bob Gruen. **80**: Iris Palmer x 2 © KJ/CD. **81**: Oxfam illustration © 2006 Nesta Fitzgerald; Laura Lauberte © KJ/CD; Thrift store in USA © BG/CD. **82**: Gloves © SSG Gloves. **83**: Lucy Macmillan-Scott © Tom Craig/CD; Lucy Granville's legs © Tom Craig/CD; Julia Jason © Lucie Layers/CD. **84**: Rita Hayworth, 1946 © Bettmann/Corbis. **85**: Pink stilettos © KJ/CD; Jimi Hendrix, 1967 © Henry Diltz/Corbis. **86**: Chloë Sevigny © 2006 Chloë Sevigny Archive; Cast of *Little House on the Prairie*, 1970 © Bettmann/ Corbis. **87**: Skateboarder, 1986 © Bettmann/Corbis; Marlene Dietrich, 1930 © Hulton-Deutsch Collection/Corbis. **88**: Chloë Sevigny © 2006 Chloë Sevigny Archive; Chloë Sevigny & Harmony Korine © 2006 Chloë Sevigny Archive. **89–90**: Chloë Sevigny x 5 © 2006 Chloë Sevigny Archive. **91**: Laura Lauberte © KJ/CD. **92**: Hands with skull rings © Norbert Huettermann/Corbis; Helen Willis Moody, 1929 © Condé Nast Archive/ Corbis. **93**: Queen Elizabeth II, 1986 © Tim Graham/Corbis; Anita Pallenberg © BG/CD; Mischa Barton © 2006 Condé Nast Archive/Regan Cameron; Nana Aganovich in straw hat © Tom Craig/CD; Woman with cowboy hat © image100/Corbis; Daisy de Villeneuve © Jan de Villeneuve; Cossack hat © Jolliffe Archive; Young skier in a fur hat, 1974 © Dean Conger/Corbis; Bay with headscarf © Garnett Archive; Chloë Sevigny © BG/CD; Grace Jones, 1982 © Lynn Goldsmith/Corbis; Tara Subkoff © BG/CD. **94**: Vicky Barron's bag stall at Portobello Market, London © KJ/CD. **95**: Selection of shoes © KJ/CD; Black high heel illustration © 2006 Lucie Layers; Black lace-up dancing shoe © Marks & Spencer Image Library. **96**: Camilla Nickerson © Mark Lebon. **97**: Belts © CD; Anita Pallenberg © BG/CD. **98**: Iris Palmer © Iris Palmer; Purple Heart © 2006 Lucie Layers. **99**: Senegalese women © Tom Craig; Karen Elson © Karl Lagerfeld; Niki Jolliffe © Jolliffe Archive; Music hall artiste Gabrielle Deslys © Hulton-Deutsch Collection/Corbis; Bonnie McCone's hand © KJ/CD; Maasai tribeswoman © Brian A. Vikander/Corbis; Bay's ring © KJ/CD; Queen Elizabeth II, 1987 by Tim Graham © Getty Images. **100**: Actress Esther Ralson © Michael Nicholson/Corbis; Laura Lauberte 2006 © KJ/CD; Diana Ross 1968 © Bettmann/Corbis. **101**: Julia Jason 2006 © Lucie Layers/CD; Socks courtesy of American Apparel, Inc.; Senegalese baby © Tom Craig. **102**: Kelis © Matthew Williamson. **103**: Kelis © Patrick Demarchelier; Linda Evans © Corbis/Sygma. Tina Turner © Bob Gruen. **104**: Yellow jeans © courtesy of Annabel Astor; Brooke Shields © Douglas Kirkland/Corbis. **105**: Ieva Imsa © KJ/CD. **106**: Iris Palmer © Tom Craig/CD **107**: Angela Davis © Sophie Bassouls/ Corbis. Tanya Tucker (in cutoffs) © Lynn Goldsmith/Corbis; Tara © Poppy de Villeneuve/CD; Senegalese woman © Tom Craig; Oonagh O'Hagen © Tom Craig/CD; Nana Oforiatta-Ayim © Poppy de Villeneuve/CD; Francesca in office © CD. **109**: Laura Lauberte x 2 © KJ/CD; Iris Palmer © KJ/CD; Tara Subkoff © Annabel Mehran; Joan Collins, 1958 © Bettman/Corbis; Eastern woman © Chris Ranier; Catherine Deneuve, 1966 © Hulton-Deutsch/Corbis. **110**: Melanie Griffith, 1988 © Lynn Goldsmith/Corbis; Pope John Paul II, 1979 © Bettmann/Corbis. **111**: Angela Buttolph © Angela Buttolph Archive; Mr Benn image by arrangement with Clive Juster & Associates © 2007 David McKee; Cheap Date pinup tent © Nick Rosen. **112**: Gloria Swanson in dress made of steel from scrapped battleships, 1922 © Bettmann/Corbis; Johnny Depp & Kate Moss, 1994 © Schwartzwald Lawrence/Corbis Sygma. **113**: Miss Piggy: TM & © The Muppets Studio, LLC. All Rights Reserved. Interview written by Miss Piggy as told to Jim Lewis. **114**: Actresses Rita Carewe and Dolores Del Rio, 1925 © John Springer Collection/Corbis; Julia Jason © Lucie Layers/CD. **115**: Screaming Lord Sutch, leader of the Official Monster Raving Loony Party, 1970 by Keystone/Stringer © Getty Images; Zac Posen © Zac Posen; Bella Freud © Tom Craig/CD. **116**: Anna Piaggi © BG/CD. **117**: Prince, 1986 © Neal Preston/Corbis; Niki and Maia Jolliffe x 2 © Jolliffe Archive; Niki Jolliffe © Jolliffe Archive; Frances Armstrong-Jones © Tom Craig/CD; Karen Elson © Karl Lagerfeld. **118**: Laura Lauberte © KJ/CD; Aurora Papafava © Michael Austin. **119**: Laura Lauberte © KJ/CD; Orsola & Uscha © Lucie Layers/CD; Karen Elson © Karl Lagerfeld. **120**: Anita Pallenberg © CD; Jeanne Moreau, 1976 © Bettmann/Corbis. **121**: Elizabeth Taylor as Cleopatra © Corbis; Joan Crawford, c.1925 © Hulton-Deutsch Collection/Corbis. **122**: Anita Pallenberg & Keith Richards © Anita Pallenberg Archive. **123**: Sam Giancana, 1957 © Bettmann/Corbis; Anita Pallenberg, Mick Jagger & Keith Richards, 1968 © Hulton-Deutsch Collection/Corbis. **124**: Carmelite Nun Edith Stein © Bettmann/Corbis; Anita Pallenberg © Tara Subkoff. **125**: Cinderella illustration, 1967 © Janet & Anne Grahame Johnstone. **Endpapers**: Leopard print spats by John Kirby, 1959 © Hulton-Deutsch Collection/ Corbis; Legs, c.1979. Image © Andy Warhol Foundation/Corbis. Artwork: © The Andy Warhol Foundation for the Visual Arts/Corbis.

Cover: Ieva Imsa photographed by Kira Jolliffe

Back Cover (top, left to right): Niki Kira Jolliffe © Jolliffe Archives; Nana Oforiatta-Ayim © BG/CD; Anita Pallenberg © BG/CF; Cheap Date pinup tent © Nick Rosen; (below): Laura Lauberte © KJ/CD.

Every effort has been made to obtain the necessary permissions with reference to copyright material, both illustrative and quoted. We apologize for any omissions in this respect and will be pleased to make the appropriate acknowledgments in any future edition.

(CD = Cheap Date, BG = Bay Garnett, KJ = Kira Jolliffe)

Thank you

A very special thanks to Lucie Layers for her tremendous contribution to this book. She has dedicated many months of work and countless appreciated opinions, and she pulls off a biker jacket brilliantly.

The *Cheap Date Guide to Style* muses: Lucy Granville, Charlotte Cooper, Jade Parfitt, Indra Jones, Verity Pemberton, Lucy Wood, Alexandra Hill, Rowan MacKinnon, Madalena Hello Kitty, Ellie Swain, Isabel at MBA, Helen Wells, Nicole Goldstein, Jenny Dyson, Henny Channon, Goshka Macuga, Minnie Weisz, Oonagh O'Hagen, Jo Weinberg, Tibbs Jenkins, Helen Evenden, Hadley Freeman, Nora Meyer, Natalie Press, Devika, Monica, Katie Morgan-Jones, Jane Pitts, Iain Aitch, Sarah Lovejoy, Daphne Hall, Prudence Beecroft, Adam Friedburg, Gustav Temple, Uscha Pohl, Orsola de Castro, From Somewhere, Saskia Spender, Sarah Vine, Sara Richardson, Anna Maconochie, Rebecca Ward, Yadira Grant, Candy Says (www.candysays.co.uk), Amanda Burns, Fanny Johnstone, Laura Hill, Angela, Daisy Garnett, Cathy Kasterine, Tarka Cordell, Matthew Grant, Aurora Papafava, Lilian Simonsson, Ramona Rainey, Paz Reussi, Kerry Haynes, Alix Eve, Saffron Aldridge, Cora Dawson, Fr. Gillean Craig, Aimee McWilliams, Courtney Clelland, Simon Murphy, Aya Imura, Annabel Mehran, Mercedes Grower, Katherine Agger, Brooke Vermillion-Tong, Serenella, Asbjorg Dunker, Wendy James (www.theracineworld.com), Sarah Skade, Isis Hjorth, Helen Watkins, Jerry Hall, Ruth Abrams, Shani Blich, Erin O'Connor, Oliver Dewey, Gina Birch, Julia Jason, Jessica Hannan, Rose Garnett, Henry, Catherine Tennant, Chloë Austerberry, Nesta Fitzgerald, Ieva Imsa and Laura Lauberte, clothes and costume designers and co-founders of Sviatsky and Jacobson.

Many thanks for the help of: Willie Burlington, James Hanson, Zandy Forbes, Andy Garnett, Cecilia Dean, Maia Dickson, Gray Jolliffe, Niki Jolliffe, Jim Jolliffe, Claire Conville, Dan Ross, Paul Sevigny, Mel Agace, Alex Shulman, Fran Bentley, Nana Oforiatta-Ayim, Robin Derrick, Connie Woodhouse, Sophie Baudrandt, Matthieu Laurette, Debbie McClellan, Bill May, Bob Gruen, Mary Fellowes, Sheila Lee, Mary Brown, Juergen Teller, Luella Bartley, Sam Pelly, Poppy de Villeneuve, Patrick Demarchelier, Regan Cameron, Phillip Ward, Corinne Day, Claire Alves, Estate of Quentin Crisp, Box Studios, Honey Luard, MBA Literary Management, Philip Lord, Jennifer Cargey.

Special thanks to: Iris Palmer, Danny Sangra for his Cheap Date letters, Jaime Perlman, Mari Roberts, Zoe Hood, Polly Devlin, British *Vogue*, Japanese *Vogue*, *V* Magazine, Karl Lagerfeld and House of Chanel.

Picture permissions sought with help from Pedro Etchegaray. Studio photographs shot at Jasmine Photographic Studios, 186-188 Shepherds Bush Road, London W6 7NL. Thank you to everyone there.

Extra-special thanks to: Susan Smith, Ben Weaver, Sarah Emsley, Neal Brown, Tom Craig, Gail Haslam, Billy Craig, Theodora Brown, Caitlin Leffel.

Cheers to Charles Miers and Universe, our US publisher.